The 500 Best Jobs— Where They'll Be and How to Get Them

MARVIN J. CETRON
WITH
MARCIA APPEL

An invaluable guide to where the 500 best jobs will be in the next twenty years, *Jobs of the Future* covers employment prospects in all major fields. Using the data bank of his internationally known company, Forecasting, International, Dr. Marvin Cetron forecasts a boom of hundreds of thousands of new positions that will be created by the present high-tech revolution that is leaving no industry or profession unaffected. *Jobs of the Future* predicts which industries are on the wane and which on the rise and simultaneously gives workers and managers a preview of new careers, employment trends, and a new computer/space age society in the making. Dr. Cetron identifies new positions in fields such as health and medicine, genetic, bionic, and laser engineering, computers and entertainment, manufacturing, geriatrics and social work, energy, environmental and hazardous waste management, communications and business, and retraining and reeducating the work force.

Dr. Cetron provides descriptions of future jobs that will be the counterparts of today's best-paying positions and how

(continued on back flap)

JOBS OF THE FUTURE

ALSO BY DR. MARVIN CETRON:

Encounters with the Future: A Forecast of Life

into the 21st Century

(with Thomas O'Toole)

JOBS OF THE FUTURE

THE 500 BEST JOBS— WHERE THEY'LL BE AND HOW TO GET THEM

by Marvin Cetron

with *MARCIA APPEL*

McGRAW-HILL BOOK COMPANY

*New York • St. Louis • San Francisco • Bogotá
Guatemala • Hamburg • Lisbon • Madrid • Mexico
Montreal • Panama • Paris • San Juan • São Paulo
Tokyo • Toronto*

1 2 3 4 5 6 7 8 9 D O C D O C 8 7 6 5 4

ISBN 0-07-010342-9

LIBRARY OF CONGRESS CATALOGING IN PUBLICATION DATA

Cetron, Marvin J.
Jobs of the future.
1. Vocational guidance.   2. Occupations—Forecasting.
I. Appel, Marcia.   II. Title.
HF5381.C422   1984   331.12'8   83-26798
ISBN 0-07-010342-9

Book design by Christine Aulicino.

For my parents, Gertrude and Jack, who taught me the dignity of work; for my colleagues, who taught me the enjoyment of work; and for my wife and kids, who taught me the necessity of work.

—Marv

To my parents, John and Retta, who always worked with me, not against me.

—Marcia

Acknowledgments

Any book that offers information about the future and jobs requires massive amounts of information from a wide variety of sources. We give special thanks to Vince Giorgi, a Minnesota writer and reporter who shared in culling, writing and editing this book, and to the Forecasting International staff for their technical and administrative support. We want to thank Thomas O'Toole of the *Washington Post*, co-author of *Encounters with the Future*, who supplied us with many meaningful insights into the labor market of the future.

We appreciate the help and foresight of Clyde Helms, president of Occupational Forecasting, a subsidiary of Forecasting International, who aided in the generation of some of the new job titles and salute him as a pioneer in recognizing the importance of watching job trends.

So many organizations and individuals provided us with facts and figures, particularly Gladys Santo of the American Vocational Association, "The Selective Guide to Colleges 1982–1983" by Edward B. Fiske, the Bureau of Labor Statistics, the National Academy of Science, and Adam Cetron, who spent many hours collecting and correlating data contained in the appendices.

Finally, we thank McGraw-Hill editor Leslie Meredith, who guided our work when we needed it most, and our agent, Ann Buchwald, for bolstering our spirits and sharpening our thoughts.

For the encouragement and many contributions of these people we would like to express our sincere gratitude. Naturally, the authors accept responsibility for any errors of fact or logic that might appear.

Contents

Introduction
A JOB
FOR THE
FUTURE...
WITH
A FUTURE

The American Dream begins and ends with a job. Working means money, a home, a car, vacations, entertainment, education for the kids, a secure retirement.

Attitudes about work change just like anything else. During the Great Depression of the 1930s, generating new jobs headed the country's list of priorities as people lost their houses, farms, cars and furniture—and their futures. But by the time the high-growth, high-productivity and high-consumption years of the 1960s arrived, attention had turned to social issues, youth dropout rates, and anti-establishment views about work and its worth.

And then the 1970s and early 1980s brought us high inflation, tough worldwide competitors, the deepest manufacturing recession since the Great Depression, and electronic machinery that blasted our American work force into a new era tinged with sci-fi wonders. Those years walloped us with the highest unemployment rates we'd experienced in the last four decades.

Now, suddenly, jobs are important again. Everyone wants a job and keeps looking for a better one all the time. To be a working man or woman is to have a ticket for the American Dream, to have a future. Getting and keeping a job with a future is everyone's number one priority.

The doomsayers are still predicting negative employment patterns and a slowly diminishing unemployment rate. But there is another side to those figures: For the first time, more than 102 million Americans are working each day. In the last two decades, the American marketplace absorbed millions of first-time workers, primarily women and teenagers and the last of the baby boom generation. And while some of the old jobs disappear each day, new ones spring up around us daily as well. Part of the work phenomenon is that people in general are interested in what the employment trends are, what they mean and how knowledge of them can be used to benefit society, business and workers themselves. *Where* you get a job and *how* you get a job require some new tactics and abilities these days. We'll concern ourselves with these new trends in this book, and point you toward getting—and keeping—a job with a future.

While there are no seers, crystal balls or mystics to accurately predict the future, understanding trends and developing personal forecasts is easier now. The Information Age that is so drastically altering our workplace also can give the average individual information to help him or her shape a safe, sane and reasonably secure future. By knowing what to look for and what to do when we find it, the job search can be more fruitful, less fearful. Once we are armed with information and a plan, the next years until 2000 can be the best part of this century rather than the Big Brother-controlled environment foretold in the classic book by Orwell, *1984.*

In this book we look at various sectors of the workplace—the factory, the office, the service industries, entertainment and communications and high-tech occupations—explain how and why they have changed and what jobs will be growth-oriented into the 21st century. Each chapter includes a listing of potential jobs—many of them brand new—and includes their definitions, educational requirements, growth potential and beginning and midcareer salary ranges. Those ranges serve as a benchmark against which to measure; maximum levels vary, of course, according to company, geographic location, experience.

When you dig into the world of work, some surprising revelations come to the surface. Here are some startling facts about U.S. industries and workers:

- U.S. industries already face a 10 to 20 percent annual shortage of well-qualified engineering school graduates;
- By 1990, only one of every five U.S. jobs will be filled by factory workers;
- Biotechnology will be one of the fastest-growing fields with the single greatest effect on your life in the next 20 years;
- The country will require over 3,000,000 CAD engineering software specialists in the next 10 years;
- Nearly 4 percent of all workers will be in some kind of job training program each year.

If you knew most of this information, move to the head of the forecasters class. If you didn't, the revelations in the following chapters can shed some light on the new world of work and help you make some clearer decisions about what you can do with the rest of your life. Whether you're a student still searching for the right occupational avenue or a white-collar or blue-collar worker suddenly thrust out of the mainstream, we've gathered information and made forecasts so you can start anticipating rather than reacting to change. We're predicting good things for job seekers who have the skills to plan for, find and perform a job.

We didn't rely on wishful thinkers, tarot cards or horoscopes for this information. It flowed in from major employers, economists, government agencies, social service agencies, social service leaders, news analyses, and was analyzed by Forecasting International, a consulting firm in Arlington, Virginia, headed by one of the book's authors, Marvin J. Cetron. We offer a list of jobs based on these indicators that could improve your odds for a good career.

When you look at the new jobs we should be seeing between now and the 21st century, you'll notice that often the training requirements are very similar. The reason for this sameness is that many of the new jobs are based on computer technology. So by understanding a computer, how to operate it, how to gather, retrieve and write the information, you may well have a foundation for several job titles. On-the-job training will provide more specialized training in a particular field.

Most of the new jobs we've included are in demand now, as is the training for them. If you're uncertain about where or whether a certain job exists, check with state agencies and employment offices that have information about jobs in demand in the marketplace. An appendix following these chapters lists vocational sources. (Also check with your state department of education, state job services agencies and state labor departments.) As you read through the listings, you'll also notice some jobs that are familiar. Many existing areas of employment will continue to enjoy average to strong growth, and, if your interest lies in one of them, you should feel confident about training for it.

We also tell you what won't work in years to come. Some service jobs, for example, will be plentiful but so low-paying that they should serve only as entry points to the job market.

Before you proceed to the first set of job listings in Chapter 1, you might want to mull over some of the major changes we spotted in the workplace and the changes we're expecting to see shortly.

AMERICANS ON THE MOVE

Shifting and sometimes confusing variations in job patterns may mean that many of us will experience a change of scenery. Just as the old American West had its ghost towns of Silver City, Leadville, Bonanza and Eureka, the industrial ghost towns of America's future will be Muncie, Detroit, Battle Creek, South Bend and many other aging industrial cities in the Northeast and Midwest.

Where will all the workers go? They'll follow the sun to the new boom states and cities: Texas, Louisiana, California, Arizona, Colorado, Utah, New Orleans, Dallas, Shreveport, Santa Fe, Houston, Los Angeles, Phoenix, Austin, San Diego. In fact, as long as water is available, the corridor of major Southern and Southwestern cities stretching from New Orleans to Los Angeles will be the new strip of influence as Philadelphia, New York, and Chicago once were. By the 21st century, however, water worries will dampen the Sun Belt's prosperity.

High tech, energy, and other major service industries will relocate heavily in these regions, but pockets of growth still will occur in some older areas like Boston (thanks to the smartest electronic network in the country around Harvard and MIT); Connecticut (the defense and high tech industries); and Minneapolis (though a deep freeze in the winter and encumbered by a high tax base, it retains a large number of homegrown and healthy Fortune 500 companies, an entrepreneurial spirit, and a dynamic combo of robust outdoor life and high culture. If the entrenched, behind-the-times Democratic-Labor-Farmer party can redefine its old liberal policies, Minneapolis has a chance of being a Midwest jewel).

Rural regions will grow not only in the Sun Belt, but also in moderate climates that promise businesses and residents reasonable energy bills year-round and an escape from big city curses. Some of the fastest growing regions in the country right now have not traditionally enjoyed prosperity in the past: the Pacific Northwest, northern California, the Sierra Nevada foothills, the Colorado Basin and the low-lying regions of the Ozark Mountains.

If you're considering a move, check to make sure the area's job rate withstood the last recession reasonably well, that the educational institutions rank high, and that the political, academic, cultural and business leadership is sound and works together.

LESS WORK, MORE PLAY AND LEARN AS YOU EARN

For the most part, the average U.S. work week has held firm at 40 hours since 1932. But a big change is finally near.

We predict that by 1990 the average worker will put in 32 hours a week and 25 hours a week by 2000. To accomplish this reduction, many employees will share jobs, arranging their own schedules through flextime plans. More people will request job sharing so they can have more time at home when the kids are little, pursue hobbies and social service activities or attend school. Many companies want to increase the number of part-time employees because it cuts down on benefit costs and protects a "core" group of employees from layoffs caused by recessions and other economic shifts.

Labor unions, already in a weakened position, will forego constant demands for more money and hold out for job security, job retraining, and shared management. To negotiate successfully for these new concerns, labor will be willing to bend on part-time employment, job sharing, and other working arrangements. Management will covet and protect its skilled work force and begin to close the deplorable gaps in wages and benefits between the upper and lower echelons. Labor will be open to bending on some issues if it shares in the profits and has stock options.

A word about unemployment: Currently, a 4.5 percent unemployment rate is considered full employment. By 1990, 8.5 percent will be the new benchmark. While a disturbing figure, remember that at any given time 3.5 percent of the work force will be in education and training programs preparing for constantly evolving new jobs. Around the country, companies and unions are closing rank (finally) to interweave training into the work routine. Last fall, American Bell and AT&T workers walked off their jobs, and one of their biggest goals was the establishment of training programs. Winning those kinds of concessions is good for labor, good for business and good for the country.

Without a doubt, maintaining a skilled work force will take an enormous amount of resources. Operating training programs in vocational, technical, academic and industrial facilities 24 hours a day will eliminate duplicating expensive programs. The training will be good only if it is for jobs with a future; up until 1979, people were still learning how to be linotype and elevator operators. Keeping America trained and working requires more foresight than that.

UNORGANIZED LABOR

It's a sign of the times, a scene reenacted at countless county fairs, union fundraisers and Labor Day picnics. Union workers and their families line up to plunk down their cash and take a few whacks with a sledge hammer at an imported automobile.

The strange but graphic ritual symbolizes American union workers' disgust and frustration over foreign competitors, whom they view as having greased the skids for a decline in American industry and organized labor. On a deeper and perhaps unrecognized level, the ceremony represents exactly the sort of mindset that organized labor should avoid if it expects to remain a powerful force in U.S. politics and economics.

For a variety of reasons—many internal, others outside labor's control—organized labor in the U.S. has suffered a string of setbacks in recent years. An economic recession that began as early as 1980 has shunted many blue collar workers to the unemployment lines and boosted jobless statistics to Depression-era levels.

Foreign competition has undoubtedly been a major contributor to the decline of several U.S. industries, including steel, textiles and autos. But at the same time, exorbitant wage demands, benefit grabs and declining productivity have tempted manufacturers to move abroad, where labor can often be had for literally pennies per hour.

In 1981, President Reagan and organized labor went eyeball to eyeball when more than 12,000 air traffic controllers walked out over demands for more pay and fewer hours. Familiar with the strategy involved in a "High Noon" confrontation, Reagan drew first, dismissing the union's membership and relying on supervisory personnel to continue operations until new recruits were trained.

Meanwhile, PATCO found itself woefully short of negotiating ammunition and the "shootout" ended in a Boot Hill burial for one of organized labor's member unions.

In an article titled "The Rise and Fall of Big Labor," *Newsweek* magazine pointed out additional signs that organized labor is in trouble. The magazine reported that in 1955 unionized workers accounted for almost 35 percent of the nation's nonagricultural labor force. Today, that figure has dropped to nearly 20 percent.

Microchip by microchip, the movement toward high technology inside the nation's factories and office buildings has whittled the need for many blue-collar workers while attempts to unionize the new breed of high tech technicians have been generally unsuccessful. According to *Newsweek,* when the American Electronics Association surveyed 738 high tech companies in 1982, only 5 percent said they employed any unionized workers.

PATCO's defeat probably stiffened the backbones of managers in other U.S. industries. When faced with union demands, many management officials are now just as likely to consider closing the plant doors as they are to opening the negotiating meeting rooms. In those cases where disputes do reach bargaining, management now seems to be holding sway. Wage and benefit concessions have become commonplace. *Newsweek* reports that in 1982, negotiated wages and benefits grew 3.2 percent, the skimpiest increase in more than a decade.

Organized labor must contend with an increasingly "suntanned" U.S. economy. Factories, jobs and people are leaving the North and Northeast for the South and West, where labor historically has received a rather cool reception.

In all, the outlook for organized labor is dicey at best. But most experts agree labor unions will survive, though perhaps not with the strength and membership they once enjoyed. What's certain is that organized labor must avoid the "car bashing mentality" of some of its members. Rather than clench its muscles, clamp shut its eyes and lash out at the coming changes and challenges, organized labor must approach the years ahead with eyes and mind open.

To gain membership, union leaders will need to keep abreast of the evolving U.S. economy. Organized labor already has indicated its ability to adapt to work force fluctuations. While membership has dropped in the United Steelworkers of America and the United Autoworkers— unions linked to two struggling industries—union membership has grown in the fast-expanding service industries.

In the near future, technological advances in the workplace will offer organized labor plenty of additional opportunities to show its flexibility. Robotics, fiber optics, teletext and other new industries will spawn a vast number of new technicians, repairers and manufacturers. Whether labor unions can attract their allegiance remains to be seen.

Union leadership also may need to rearrange its priorities when negotiting with management. By way of recognizing both the continually evolving nature of the nation's workplace and the need to keep union members employable, unions may choose to emphasize training and retraining programs along with wages and benefits. Shorter work weeks, job sharing and cooperative programs mentioned before to boost productivity are issues in which labor may take a lead.

Labor's biggest challenge might be one of public image. An increasing number of Americans look on union laborers as underworked and overpaid. Continued inflation and burgeoning unemployment have curtailed the public's patience for organized labor's wage and benefit demands. And many high tech workers are resisting unionization because they fear it will bring the declines in productivity and product quality sometimes associated with labor.

Organized labor in the United States celebrated its 100th birthday in 1981. It will take flexibility, planning and innovative leadership to keep organized labor alive for its bicentennial.

SERVICING AMERICA

One of the easiest employment trends to spot is the projected growth in service industries and service industry jobs. Take a few minutes to put down this book, open up your checkbook and scan the check register. There you'll get some idea of the broad range of service jobs which touch all facets of our lives: dry cleaning, a haircut, insurance, flowers, movie tickets, a restaurant tab, the plumber, new eyeglasses, groceries, a pizza, the babysitter, postage stamps, health club fees, television repairs, a tune-up and oil change.

Service occupations steadily have grown to become the economic roots of the U.S. work force. According to the U.S. Bureau of Labor Statistics, more than two-thirds of the nation's employment growth during the past 20 years has come in the service sector and that trend is expected to continue. The number of service jobs is expected to jump from 67.5 million in 1980 to as many as 83.5 million by 1990. By 2000, it's projected that as much as 90 percent of the U.S. labor force will work in service occupations.

Granted, this growth could be both good and bad news for anyone seeking a job, whether he or she is a student planning a future or an individual plotting a new career course. Many service jobs are traditionally poor paying, low-skilled occupations. Dishwashing, garbage collecting and shoe shining, for instance, generally are not careers to which one aspires.

But not all service sector jobs fall on the bottom end of the employment ladder. Accountants, attorneys, teachers and law enforcement officers are all part of the service sector. And as technology continues to change the way we live and work, new jobs—many requiring great skill and paying hefty salaries—will find a rung in the service group. Consider that by the year 1990 the country is expected to need about 160,000 robot technicians to service a growing family of industrial and office robots. And as the average age of the U.S. populace continues to increase, a new area of vital service work will be created to attend to the needs of the nation's elderly.

Some economists fear that the U.S. economy eventually will suffer because service jobs are replacing manufacturing jobs as the nation's employment base. But for the individual planning a career, *where* the jobs will be becomes more important than *whether* those jobs are good for the economy at large. A job seeker can only plan for where the U.S. economy is headed, not predict where it will finally end up. And to reiterate, the U.S. economy is headed toward service.

THE CONNECTION: COMPUTERS AND CABLES

By the mid-1990s, 95 percent of what we learn will be stored in computers; much of that knowledge will be learned by operating a computer. The connecting lines between the dots of the employment picture are actually microchips, integrated circuits and cable lines. Together, these communications devices, deliverers and decipherers will be responsible for job elimination, job creation, job training and job transfer.

Here's a quick example. Let's say you are the world's

foremost expert on the poetry of William Butler Yeats. Two continents away, a graduate student writing a paper about this renowned author wants to buy your knowledge to complete his task. He will find you by exploring a computer data base, then "talk" to you and make the buy electronically. If your computer or cable systems are compatible, and in the future compatibility will be a given, you will transfer your knowledge to the buyer without pen, paper, or postal service. He will send payment the same way. In fact, neither of you may have to leave your home to conduct any part of this transaction.

The first electric computer, built in a large room at the University of Pennsylvania in 1943, ran on more than 18,000 vacuum tubes. Today, a pocket calculator available on the market boasts a memory greater than its 1943 forebearer, and a desktop computer stores what 16,000 human brains can remember. By 1990, the average computer will perform 200 million operations a second, and by the 21st century, the supercalcs will do 8 billion operations a second.

Today, microcomputers are in homes and businesses balancing checkbooks and financial statements, planning menus and production schedules, storing Christmas card lists and customer service orders, teaching kids and retraining workers.

As a result of the massive power and capability of today's computers, a worldwide telecommunications industry has been launched, and with satellite and laser technology at hand, not even the sky is the limit. In 1980, telecommunications sales totalled $40 billion and are expected to soar to $160 billion by the turn of the century. This industry, the fastest-growing for the last 10 years and certainly for the next 10, will alter the way we work, learn, teach, shop, are entertained, and will allow us to have a vocabulary greater than the average person's in every language. Not even the most narrow-minded dictatorial regime will be able to dam the flow of information. Some day soon, these machines will accept, understand and carry out voice commands and recognize their "leader."

As computerized telephones and computers take their place in the home alongside cable television, workers will work at home, voters will vote at home, students will study at home. Families will form their own data bases and maybe produce their own television shows.

There's a problem underneath all this good news: unless cables and computers are distributed evenly throughout the schools and homes in the United States, the materially and intellectually rich will get richer and the poor poorer. Those who already limp along may even lose their jobs to this new giant of an industry. For example, when we can order most of our own goods from home, there will be no need for retail clerks, jobs traditionally held by young people and those lacking precise skills.

OF WOMEN, MEN AND THE GREAT ERA (EQUAL RIGHTS AMENDMENT)

Alongside robots and microchips, the decline of the smokestack industries and the growth of service jobs, one of the most powerful and dramatic forces on the labor market in the next 20 years will be the maturing influence of women. Today, women make up 48 percent of all workers and will account for most of the new entrants in the future. Almost 1 million additional women will join the work force every year through the next decade. Long before 1990, the majority of America's workers will be women.

Not only are attitudes finally changing about women's role in the marketplace, but women also are taking responsibility for their own financial support. "If you expect some guy to come in on a white horse and take care of you," Dr. Alicia Pagano, director of education for the Girl Scouts of America, said not long ago, "you're only one heartbeat away from unemployment."

Right now, more than 55 percent of all women between 25 and 44 years of age work outside the home. By 1990, we expect the percentage to jump to 85. Most working women are half of a career couple, a growing trend in the years ahead. Among the *few* jobs women won't have in the next 20 years will be as priests in the Roman Catholic, Greek, and Russian Orthodox churches.

The revolutionary trends opening up the workplace to women have been underway now for more than 10 years. Twenty years ago, women made up 25 percent of the undergraduate students in U.S. universities. In 1978, more women than men enrolled in the nation's freshman collegiate class for the first time. Today, they make up 52 percent of the total number of undergraduates. In the 1920s, only 12 in every 100 graduate students earning doctorate degrees in science and engineering were women. By 1981, 1 of every 4 doctoral degrees in science and engineering in the United States was being earned by a woman.

The same trend is being charted in the nation's business schools and law schools, once even more exclusive male abodes than science and engineering. In 1971, there were 758 women among the 21,417 students enrolled in graduate business schools and a paltry 3.5 percent of the Master's of Business Administration (MBA) candidates were females. A decade later, there were 14,500 female MBA candidates or 26 percent of the total. In the late 1960s, male law students outnumbered women, 23–1. At last count, there were 42,122 women training for the law, 34 percent of the total.

Nowhere are women making more rapid progress than in business, where the term "businessman" means nothing anymore. A 1982 American Bankers Association survey of the nation's 15 largest banks shows that 40 percent of their "officials and managers" were women, up 2 percent in a single year and more than 5 percent in 3 years. The number of female accountants has more than doubled in the last 10 years. So have women in media, advertising, and public relations. Women now make up 20 percent of the 4,100 public relations professionals with more than 5 years' experience and that number is bound to go higher, according to the Public Relations Society of America, "since 80 percent of those studying public relations in college are women." The day when women routinely run large corporations unfortunately is still a long way off, but even the doors of the executive suites are no longer slammed shut to women, who now occupy one-fourth of the managerial and administrative jobs in private industry in America.

An even more important statistic is how many women (though not enough) have become members of major corporate boards of directors. After all, says Felice Schwartz, president of Catalyst, a career think-tank for women, "Corporate directorship symbolizes upward mobility." Of the 500 largest industrial manufacturers, 173 have at least one woman director. Six of the ten largest corporations in the country have at least one woman on the board and three of the top ten have two female directors. They are Mobil, General Motors and IBM.

Women's major gains in the sciences have been in medicine, psychology and the computer sciences, where they now make up about one-third of the labor force in each of these professions.

Women have begun to move out of such traditional roles in medicine as obstetrics, pediatrics, gynecology and dermatology to challenge the male strongholds such as cardiology, orthopedics and surgery. The operating room is the male doctor's last refuge, but not for long. Between 1978 and 1980, the number of women in surgical residencies jumped 20 percent to almost 1,200. From 1971 to 1981, women making up the dental school graduating class went from 1.2 to 13.5 percent, in veterinary school from 9.4 to 32.8 percent, and in pharmacy school from unknown and unregistered to 37.5 percent.

The thrust of women into American political life has just begun. In the next 20 years, it will reach dimensions we cannot perceive today. We predict towns and suburbs will be governed by women to an extent never imagined. As an example, more than one-fourth of the New Hampshire state legislators are women and that proportion will grow to half or even two-thirds by 2000. Those political winnings will spread from Long Island to Los Angeles.

Outside of business, the law and professional sciences, women will make major gains in the next 20 years in the blue collar and service jobs almost always reserved for men because they were thought to require brawn and bravado. If there is one single development that could tilt the future in the direction of women, it's the high tech movement. Robots and computers create thousands of new tasks that simply won't require the same hand and upper-arm strength the old factory ones demanded. The high-level, high-tech jobs will open up to women too.

Studies have shown that some young girls and women don't believe they can excel in math and science, in large part because of their social and cultural conditioning. But as these attitudes disappear, more women will become data communications managers, electronic communicators and robot technicians and supervisors. More women will master technologies, math and science, which, combined with their communicating and interpersonal skills, will have great impact on future corporate cultures.

Women are about to enter what is surely the most exciting time for their gender in all history. With the arrival of computer technology and its equalizing effects, the doors stand wide open. In the new society, almost everything will be "women's work." As more women enter the marketplace and positions open up to them, working conditions will change as women will ask for and get on-site day care, schools located closer to work than home, extended vacations for fathers to share parenting demands, job-sharing time during the child-bearing years and remote technology to allow parents to work at home during emergencies. As the roles of the two genders slowly merge, so will the social and business networks link. Men and women will settle business at the club, on the squash courts, on the 19th hole. The sheer numbers of working women will inevitably change society, and, in the end, men will come to prefer it.

Finally, women must continue to push for an end to salary differentials. No matter how far they've come, women still don't make the same money and benefits as their male counterparts. The sad fact of the matter is women who are full-time, year-round workers earn only 60 cents for every dollar earned by men. Even as recently as 1981, women with five or more years of college earned less on average than men who only had high school diplomas. The Information Age could accomplish quickly what might have taken the Equal Rights Amendment decades to do.

As women become the majority members of the work force, they will start making rules. And if that doesn't do it alone, that together with the ERA will turn the tide forever. By 1989, the 50th state will ratify a substitute amendment that will be acceptable to women. By the end of the century, American women will achieve the same kind of power and freedom long ago won by the women of Sweden, who make just as much money as men, or by the women of Finland, where almost one-third of the Finnish Parliament is female.

THE JOB SEEKERS

People hunting for jobs in the future will fall into one of several categories, a trend quite different from the good old 1950s when you found a job after graduating and stayed with it.

Teenagers are going to want to bring home paychecks to finance their cars, designer clothes, music and makeup. But they'll be met by more resistance from parents and teachers who suspect that the lure of the buck and the permissiveness given kids to pursue it in the last 20 years has had a detrimental effect on their studies.

There always will be the first-time job seeker, the person who has finished college or vocational school and wants a good entry-level position with growth opportunity.

A new phenomenon is the MBA-trained graduate who thinks the degree comes complete with a junior level executive status. This theory is beginning to wear thin as these youngsters command high salaries and then still are wet behind the ears in the business world. Like lawyers, there will soon be too many of them to do anything but compete with each other for jobs.

Women entering the work force for the first time will continue to have heavy influence through the 1990s, and it is some kind of compliment to this aging economic system that so many women have moved into paying jobs. In Japan, for example, which likes to boast about it's low unemployment, women have been denied access to anything but servile job opportunities. If Japanese women ever demand more, Japan's tightly controlled economy will have a huge test to pass.

Finally, we're going to see more people than ever preparing for second, third or even fourth careers. Some will be displaced workers; others will be in natural evolutionary phases.

BUILDING A BUSINESS

While international corporations continue to gobble each other up in the name of efficiency between now and the 21st century, small businesses won't be lost in their main course.

In 1950, fewer than 100,000 new businesses took form, compared with 700,000 in 1983. Self-employment has hit boom times as well. After a 20-year decline, the number of people self-employed increased by 25 percent during the 1970s and probably will double in the next decade.

People are walking away from large institutions and structured management to smaller firms and entrepreneurship and are not turning back. The *Wall Street Journal* reports that the number of executives leaving big companies in favor of smaller ones has doubled in recent years. Execs who've made the switch say they now have more satisfaction, independence and—in some cases—more money.

We think part of the reason for this explosive growth is simply because the corporations create such waste, low productivity, confusion and paternalistic managements that small companies are essentially for cleaning up the messes and meeting demand. In fact, we predict that workers soon routinely will rank management's ability to manage from bottom up instead of top down or face employee takeovers.

Small businesses react more quickly because they have fewer layers of paranoid managers to coerce and soothe. Big companies say, "Can we sell enough of it to make it worthwhile?" Small firms must pinpoint a product to the specific needs of their customers or go broke.

We predict the movement into the Information Age will provide a fertile environment for entrepreneurs. For example, what does it take to write computer software? A cheap microcomputer and an electric outlet.

Look for new business formation to boom and, with it, look for some very successful, very happy and very rich young business owners.

BRAVE NEW WORK

The preceding trends are just a few hints of how working may change by the 21st century. More ideas, facts and suggestions can be found in the following chapters.

Basically, we remain optimistic, convinced that the soul of the worker can be triumphant over the soul of the new machine.

Jobs doesn't have to be a four-letter word, but rather an opportunity for the future.

1
OFFICE
OF
THE FUTURE

Administration, Management and Assistants

You might want to commit the following word to memory: "biotechnology"—the study of the relationship between humans and machines.

It's not that you're likely to find the word itself sprouting up during bus-stop conversations or cocktail party chit-chat. Biotechnology won't replace politics, weather and sports as topics of casual conversation.

But its subject matter will. The relationship between humans and machines—most notably the omnipresent computer—is going to be a hot topic for years to come, whether it is called by its technical name or not.

Computers are moving in, taking over and redefining the work place. And perhaps nowhere is this new "administrative assistant"—which never strolls to the water machine, never takes a java break, never goes fishing and rarely needs a sick day—expected to have a greater impact than in the offices of white-collar managers and administrators.

The "Office of the Future," some folks call this revolution. Others refer to it as "white-collar automation." Regardless of the label, the fact is at least half of the 3 million white-collar workers among the nation's unemployed today lost their jobs to automation.

If those numbers failed to get your attention, here are some more. Some economists are predicting that during the next 20 years office automation will eliminate between 30 and 50 million additional jobs from a white-collar work force which numbers about 90 million.

Now, before someone invents a new four-letter expletive for this seemingly disastrous union of people and machines, it should be noted that the Office of the Future will have a creative force as well as a destructive one on the nation's job market.

In fact, office automation should help eliminate waste, improve productivity and create thousands of new and more challenging jobs for those willing to adapt and train themselves.

It's true that machines which listen, speak, write, rewrite, correct spelling errors, store and file will largely do away with need for typists, dictationists, stenographers and even the traditional secretary. But, it's also true that office automation should free those people for other tasks likely to require more training, but also offering better pay and greater job satisfaction.

The impetus behind building the Office of the Future is productivity. During the 1970s, factory productivity soared 85 percent while office productivity nudged ahead a meager 4 percent.

The reason? Automation entered the factories where it was cheaper and easier to implement and boosted productivity. Meanwhile, without similar progress toward automation, the office continued as a clerical "bucket brigade," straining to handle a flood of information.

Electronics will streamline the process in the Office of

the Future, where, for example, messages and memos will hop from computer console to computer console, freeing office phones for important incoming calls.

The electronic storage and retrieval of information eventually will lead to the "paperless" office, increasing productivity while eliminating tedious and time-consuming typing, proofreading, editing and retyping chores.

Managers, administrators and secretaries eagerly will use desktop terminals to compile, analyze and interpret the information they need to perform their work. The touch of a button will retrieve contracts, office reports, research studies and purchase orders. "Information tracking" will become commonplace, with dunning letters automatically written and mailed to overdue accounts, quick checks made on the status of information requests and reminders moved via computer to people charged with locating answers.

Expect the desktop "Rolodex" to roll over and disappear. Telephone numbers and addresses will be stored in the computer, which will also check spellings and maintain a calendar of meetings, luncheons, appointments, out-of-town trips, birthdays and anniversaries.

In addition, automation will bring us "electronic mail," which employs computers, communications satellites and rooftop microwave antennas to send messages, letters, mailgrams, voicegrams and picturegrams across the country and around the globe.

The office telephone is likely to be replaced by a 12-key, pushbutton "cousin" that receives and holds calls, records the time and length of calls and displays phone numbers on a small screen. Computerized switchboards may replace the office switchboard operators. They also will run alarm systems and smoke detectors and monitor heat and air flow for maximum energy efficiency throughout an office building.

Computerized voice machines sooner than later will take dictation, read the letter back, type it, proofread, make corrections and retype. The National Security Agency and at least three major corporations already are testing the first generation of these machines. So far, they have proved to be 92 percent accurate, making mistakes only when the person dictating coughs, sneezes or slurs a word.

Such revolutionary developments in electronic technology will clearly have tremendous impact, not only in the office but in many other areas of commerce.

Electronic telemarketing will alter radically the way we shop. It will no longer be necessary to hop in the car, drive to a local shopping center and pick out a rug, a chair or perhaps even groceries.

Instead, a consumer will scan an electronic catalog, a video screen displaying product information and pictures before phoning an order in to a telemarketing center. There, a customer order recording specialist will take the request, check the inventory, confirm the purchase and relay the purchase order to the billing and shipping departments.

Telemarketing will not only simplify shopping, but also generate hundreds of thousands of new jobs during the next 20 years. And in defense of the intimate relationship between humans and machines, the jobs will be created because of electronic automation, not in spite of it.

Computers will play an equally important role in manufacturing, design and advertising. A computer-aided design draftsman will use computerized blueprints to compose final blueprints of automobiles, airplanes, appliances, and more. Similarly, a computer-assisted graphics and layout artist will use computers to lay out pages for newspapers, magazines, advertisements, books and almost any other printed material.

In all, it's projected that electronics and automation should create about 10.5 million new white-collar jobs in the next 10 years alone. The new jobs, unlike the semi-skilled tasks of the past like typing and filing, will demand more education, training and retraining.

They'll have job titles like computer graphics technician, computer drafting technician, computer layout artist, terminal information processor and advertising sales programmer.

American Telephone and Telegraph already is gearing itself and its employees for the training necessary to gain jobs in the Office of the Future. AT&T now spends $1 billion annually for training and retraining its 1.1 million white collar workers. AT&T estimates that each office employee will have at least five different jobs in his or her career with the company.

We all might be wise to learn from the attitude of AT&T toward office automation—fear not, be prepared and stay flexible.

The door to the Office of the Future is already ajar and swinging rapidly open. The following list includes more than 40 jobs which wait just behind that door.

Job Title	Job Numbers	Starting $	Mid $	Education
Computer Software Writer	1,830,000	$20,000	$30,000	2–4 years college

Someone has to get the ball, or in this case the chip, rolling and design the programs that instruct the computers to perform a variety of functions in chemistry labs, hospitals, law offices, engineering departments and business offices.

| Computer Graphics Technician | 150,000 | $20,000 | $35,000 | 2 years college |

Uses computers to design graphs, charts, pie charts, bar charts, work tables, any mechanism for showing percentage gains, losses and differences. Could work on quarterly and annual reports for corporations, budgets and payroll breakdowns for universities and government, or graphics to illustrate new reports for television, newspapers and magazines.

| Computer Drafting Technician | 300,000 | $18,000 | $30,000 | 2 years college |

Uses computers to prepare the equivalent of blue-prints for architects, surveyors, engineers, and systems analysts. Display consoles will soon be able to show blue-prints in three dimensions and with better precision than the best traditional blueprints. Will convert the rough drawings of architects and engineers into finished plans so workers can use them to produce engines, machinery, aircraft and buildings.

Computer- Assisted Graphics Layout Artist	40,000	$10,000	$18,000	2 years college/ 2 years voca- tional

Uses computers to lay out pages of newspapers, magazines, reports, periodicals, books or almost anything else in print. Will use colors, three-dimensional graphics as computer aids to border printed sections of pages, advertising layouts and periodical supplements. Will work for newspapers, magazines, advertising agencies, book publishers, commercial artists, record companies (record jackets), brochures and catalogues.

Computer- Assisted Graphics (CAG) Terminal Input Artist	40,000	$16,800	$30,000	2 years college/ 2 years voca- tional

Uses computers to compose typefaces, lettering, designs on packages and also integrate art, lettering and backgrounds that enhance packaging. Will work solely at a computer terminal, taking direction from layout artist. Will work for an advertising agency or in the marketing department of corporations that retail their products in supermarkets and department stores.

CAG Sales Represen- tative	30,000	$15,000	$30,000	2 years voca- tional

A new kind of salesperson. Will help merchants and customers select the right kinds of computer machinery that will allow them to use computerized graphics in their business. Must be familiar with all phases of computer hardware.

CAG Operations Supervisor	20,000	$15,000	$25,000	2 years voca- tional

Ensures that schedules are met on time, jobs are done at cost and interact with people in the most productive fashion. Must have at least a working knowledge of computer graphics.

Computer- Aided Design (CAD) Terminal Draftsman	300,000	$14,000	$25,000	2 years college/ 2 years voca- tional

Uses computerized blueprints of separate machinery parts to incorporate all designs into one product. For instance: takes blueprints of a car engine, chassis, frame, windshield, etc. to draw up (using the computer) a design for an entire automobile.

CAD Product Design Technician	190,000	$14,700	$28,000	2 years college/ 2 years voca- tional

Takes the product of the design draftsman (listed above) and puts it all together to work out sizes, dimensions, where parts connect. Also takes engineering designs and puts them in proper formats for a computer to assimilate into one complete blueprint. Will work on all types of large machinery and structures, from automobiles to bridges.

CAD Product Engineer	600,000	$14,500	$35,000	4 years college

Uses the computerized blueprints of the technicians and draftsmen and applies theories and principles of engineering to the practical end product. Decides on materials, substitute materials, heat resistant parts, drag resistant frames and shapes for the most economical performance of the product. Needs to know computer graphics as well as conventional engineering.

CAD Parts Cataloguer	125,000	$11,000	$17,500	2 years vocational

Uses computers and an enormous computerized index to locate small and large machine and materials parts for designers, manufacturers and builders. Updates inventory changes, parts modifications and substitutions to cut costs and speed deliveries.

CAD Information Retrieval and Reproduction Clerk	300,000	$9,500	$12,000	high school

The future replacement for the old clerical file clerk. Will not do filing. Instead will compose a list of indexed "key words" where computers have filed documents and information and then be able to retrieve it and pass it on to the people requiring it. Will work in any white collar office where files must be maintained.

CAD Engineering Software Specialist	360,000	$19,000	$35,000	2 years college

Writes the computer-aided design software, which instructs the computers to turn out work when directed. If working in an automobile engineering lab, will have to understand how windshields are fitted into cars, how they're shaped and how windshield wiper blades are designed to best fit the windshield. Each time a car model changes, will have to rewrite the software instructions for the computer to adapt to the change. This person takes the engineer's ideas and designs them into a software program.

CAD Training Software Specialist	150,000	$14,500	$19,000	2 years college/ 2 years vocational

Will develop software training instructions to help prepare future software specialists like those in the job described above. Also acts as a teacher who must not only understand software procedural changes but also instruct people in classroom environments and on-the-job situations to give students their best shot for the real thing.

CAD Sales Trainer	95,000	$12,500	$19,800	2 years college/ 2 years vocational

Will train people to sell the computer-aided design machinery and software packages. Customers will be across-the-board computer-aided design users, ranging from engineers who design aircraft and appliances to the consultants who work at home building a better lawnmower. Will work for computer hardware and software manufacturers.

Computer-Assisted Manufacturing and CAD Software Coordinator	80,000	$14,000	$24,000	2 years vocational

Will work to "mesh" the software instructions for the programs that design individual parts for such items as a motor or an appliance. If working for a manufacturer of air conditioners, will coordinate software instructions for the compressor, the condensor, the fan motor that cools the air and the blow motor that passes the cool air to the consumer so all are integrated in the program that puts the entire cooling system together.

Computer Information Processor	270,000	$20,000	$30,000	2 years college

Not a software writer, but an editor. Decides how information will be collected, in what order it can be retrieved and in what form it comes out. Will it be the word "two" or the number "2"? Determines for the software writer what will be in the writer's program. Translates for the software writer the user's needs.

| Computer Distributive Information Processor | 140,000 | $20,000 | $35,000 | 2 years college |

The computerized traffic cop. Responsible for setting up and monitoring electronic mail systems, electronic funds transfer systems, etc. Gets the electronic receipts to make sure everything was delivered the right way. Equivalent of the old-fashioned mailroom supervisor, only this person guarantees the *electronic* information keeps moving. His enemies aren't snow, sleet or rain, but rather computer bugs, down-time and overload.

| Telemarketing Advertising and Scenario Writer | 110,000 | $18,000 | $35,000 | 4 years college |

Helps plan and execute advertising programs that will be carried over cable television and picture telephones. Also writes the advertising copy.

| Advertising and Sales Programmer | 65,000 | $25,000 | $85,000 | 4 years college |

Determines telemarketing strategy, tactics, approaches to test markets, how to sample products electronically and what kinds of products to sample on the air. The sales and marketing directors of the past.

| Camera, Sound Technician, Camera Technician | 50,000 | $25,000 | $40,000 | 2 years college |

Will set up graphics displays. Sound technicians integrate and synchronize the music and words that will accompany the graphics. Much more training received on-the-job.

Customer Order Recording Specialist	80,000	$15,000	$19,000	2 years college

The stock clerk's electronic clone. Will take orders by phone, use computer to check inventory, order the item if it's in stock, and backfill the order if it's not. Passes on the purchase order electronically to the billing and shipping offices.

Operations Analyst	60,000	$17,500	$22,500	2 years college

Will plan, schedule and coordinate all activities in the telemarketing system. He's the operations director, the systems analyst, the executive officer on a naval vessel, the director of plans at the CIA.

Shipping, Billing Clerk	50,000	$7,500	$17,500	2 years vocational

The electronic "equal" of the shipping and billing clerk. Deals with electronic machines instead of bills of lading and will need a rudimentary understanding of computers.

Teletext Cable TV Liaison	30,000	$17,500	$38,000	2 years vocational

Coordinates between correspondents and editors at the start of the news flow and the television station broadcasting the "teletext." Remember: in teletext there are no pictures. This is the teleprompter of the future.

| Marketing Specialist | 30,000 | $18,500 | $40,000 | 4 years college |

Similar to the familiar market analyst except the specialist also will analyze the reasons people are buying products through the teletext channels. He will tell his pitchmen which trends are the strongest.

| Software Program Development Specialist | 30,000 | $18,500 | $27,500 | 2 years vocational |

Develops software instructions for the cheapest, quickest and easiest way to reach listeners and viewers via teletext.

| Operations Supervisor | 25,000 | $20,000 | $34,000 | 2 years vocational |

Floor manager for the teletext office. Assures deadlines are met, software is working, cables are connected. The electronic foreman of the future.

| Librarian's Supervisor | 20,000 | $18,300 | $25,500 | 4 years college |

Collects and disseminates research, handles teleconference calls in some offices, verifies the authenticity of the research.

| Broadcast Engineer | 25,000 | $18,500 | $27,000 | 4 years college |

Does the same job as television engineers do today except for teletext. No concern about lighting and camera angles but worries about images lining up precisely, colors blending, and background music and voiceovers matching.

| Assistant Editor | 50,000 | $18,000 | $25,000 | 4 years college |

Writes, not edits, the rough draft texts for the message. The same person 10 to 20 years ago wrote for radio news announcers. Now will have to consider how the words look rather than how they sound.

| Editor, Operations Director | 25,000 | $30,500 | $50,000 | 4 years college |

Does some writing, lots of rewriting, but really plans the contents of the teletext news broadcast or advertising message. Assigns topics to writers and oversees production of all teletext programs. The producer, the director, the boss.

| Automated Office Message Center Manager | 300,000 | $16,000 | $28,000 | 4 years college |

Runs the nerve center of the automated office, its message center. Gets all incoming electronic mail and message traffic and routes it. A brand new job.

| Terminal Operator | 600,000 | $14,500 | $23,400 | 2 years college |

Tomorrow's word processor, a person who needs two years of college to learn the computerized system, its shortcomings and strengths. Will be expected to improve on everybody else's spelling and knowledge of household words, geographic locations and everyday information gleaned from newspapers.

| Information Security Manager | 260,000 | $18,000 | $25,000 | 4 years college |

The electronic floorwalker in the department store, the house detective in the hotel and the electronic counter-intelligence officer of the future. Responsible for protecting proprietary, personal and classified data stored on memory banks. Develops and changes codes and uses electronic scrambling devices to safeguard the office's electronic secrets. The James Bond of the information world; perhaps the most exciting job in the Office of the Future.

| Information-Manage-ment Director | 150,000 | $22,500 | $50,000 | 4 years college |

The Office Manager of the Future. Responsible for analyzing the information coming from the field, customers and clients and distributing it.

| Work Station Manager | 240,000 | $18,000 | $25,000 | 2 years vocation |

Responsible for all data going into an office's information system. Like the manager of today's typing pool except that the job will be a lot tougher and more demanding. Will manage more machines than people and more types of machines than people.

| Productivity Analyst | 100,000 | $14,500 | $22,500 | 4 years college |

The efficiency expert of the future, the time-study person who made sure the company was getting the most from its people. Will have more machines to watch and fewer people to supervise than his counterpart of the past. Must make sure people are using the best available machines.

Work Systems Technician	180,000	$14,100	$19,800	2 years voca- tional

Responsible for office happiness in the electronic Office of the Future. Will make sure the machines are compatible with people. Are the console color screens the best? Can the person at the console better work at home rather than in the office?

Data Manage- ment Analyst	250,000	$15,500	$25,000	4 years college

Makes sure there is no "information pollution" or overload in the electronic office. Though it's paperless, the Office of the Future could become overloaded with electronic data. This worker decides what's needed and what isn't.

Economist	44,000	$20,000	$45,000	4 years college

Will attempt to discover solutions to a variety of economic questions and problems which crop up in the course of conducting business and commerce. Includes research, preparing findings and suggesting plans and alternatives to client. More advanced economic theorists will need graduate work.

Personnel Adminis- trator	405,000	$28,000	$50,000	4 years college

Supervise all facets of employment, including hiring and firing, performance evaluations, interviews. Also charged with administering a variety of employee programs, including training, insurance, etc. Finding qualified personnel for a continually changing work place will be both challenging and necessary.

Bank Officers and Administrator	643,000	$16,000	$29,000	4 years college

Acts as manager and overseer of bank departments, including credit, trust and loan divisions. Officers direct the bank within a policy structure established by the board of directors.

Blue Collar Worker Supervisor	1,300,000	$16,000	$19,000	2 years vocational

Covers a wide variety of supervisory positions, most commonly referred to as foremen and forewomen.

City Manager	4,000	$33,000	$49,000	4 years college

Responsible for the day-to-day administration of a city. Population growth in both the West and South should create demand for "sun belt" city managers, especially. Look for more regional planning as areas share scarce resources and boundaries become less important. Salaries vary with city size.

Urban and Regional Planning Specialist	23,000	$22,000	$32,000	4 years college

Develops plans to handle the future growth of an urban area. Also advises local officials on a broad range of problem areas, including waste handling, sewer and water systems, street planning, housing, construction and more. Old cities will require planners with expertise in rehabilitation and modernization. Rural areas must cope with "sprawl" from acreages.

Sales Represen- tative, Wholesale	1,001,000	$18,000	$33,000	4 years college

Sells products to stores, which in turn sell to consumers. Involves visiting buyers, displaying product samples and in general "pitching" a product to buyers.

Adminis- trative Assistant	1,000,000	$11,500	$28,500	2 years college

Even with the advent of office automation, many executives and administrators will need a "right hand human" to help coordinate various duties.

As we noted earlier, the electronic advances we've discussed will eliminate some jobs—and not solely clerical positions.

Business Week magazine points out that middle managers—who advise top executives on strategic planning, marketing, engineering and other business matters—are entering a "new era." The magazine said middle management is "being turned upside down. The onrushing electronics revolution is changing the role of the middle manager and forcing radical restructuring of the corporation's middle ranks, shrinking them drastically in the best-managed companies."

Some examples of the drastic cuts in middle management during 1982–1983: Alcoa, 15 percent; Firestone, 20 percent; Crown Zellerbach, 20 percent; Chrysler, 40 percent.

The computer is gradually usurping the middle manager's role as information gatherer and analyzer. Data now flows directly from the computer memory to the executive suite without the editing, monitoring and second-guessing traditionally provided by middle managers.

For the next generation at least, retraining middle managers will be a vital task. Business schools can help in the transition by emphasizing manufacturing, marketing and computer skills more than analysis.

Business schools, in fact, may need to take a hard, calculating look at their programs for training the nation's business managers and executives. The old "bottom line" approach to business management is no longer sufficient for businesses to survive—much less flourish—in a constantly changing business environment.

Many MBA programs, for example, will need to pay greater attention to computer training so their graduates won't be intimidated by what could be their most valuable managerial tool.

George Korey, president of the Canadian School of Management, points out that it may be time to revamp the traditional educational track, which pushes young people from high school, through college, on to graduate school and out into the business world—armed with a briefcase brimming with managerial theory and little else.

In a paper presented to the World Future Society, entitled "Education for Managers of Accelerating Change," Korey noted that better coordination between the needs of the business world and the formal education of business leaders is necessary to provide top-quality managers for the future.

Korey suggests that top-flight business schools will offer credit for real-life work and managerial experience while at the same time maintaining academic excellence. He also argued that potential managers may benefit from exposure to a healthy mix of management theory and hands-on work experience. In addition, he stresses the importance of attuning managers to the needs and problems of the world around them—not just the 9-to-5 world sealed inside the glass walls of their particular corporate skyscraper. For example, many corporations are already "adopting" schools, loaning managers and technical employees to serve as teachers in an effort to bolster sagging educational systems. Also, the private sector is increasingly asked to participate in joint ventures with government and education. The Job Training Partnership Act calls for private business representatives to serve on councils that direct the training of people needing jobs.

Korey points out that such changes not only provide a sound managerial education for young people, but also meet the needs of "nontraditional" students, who, for a variety of reasons, require additional formal education even though they already possess a wealth of practical knowledge.

Finally, Korey notes that future managers may need some training in the area on which this book is based—peering into the future. By studying current trends and making educated hypotheses about the future, managers may steer their companies toward serene and profitable "waters" and avoid some of the stormy seas which have swamped steel, auto and a number of other U.S. industries.

Future managers also will need to understand the notion of retraining—what many refer to as "investing in human capital." With technology changing the work environment on a nearly daily basis, retraining will be a necessity to meet business demands while hanging on to valued employees.

Before we turn out the lights on the Office of the Future, it should be stressed again that electronics will help improve office productivity by eliminating waste and drudgery inherent in many traditional office tasks. By ridding the white collar work world of the drudgery, office automation will offer workers greater control over their lives and provide more opportunity for job satisfaction.

In studies of Sweden's male, white-collar employees, Robert Karasek of New York's Columbia University discovered that those with the least control over their work were the most susceptible to mental depression and cardiovascular disease. He found that workers with greater control over their jobs had less illness and longer lifespans. And Karasek's study also revealed a link between worker autonomy and the successful pursuit of social and leisure activity, which in turn promoted physical and mental well being among workers.

Office automation, by turning mundane tasks over to machines, frees people to create, imagine, direct, lead, excel—things no computer can do.

2
SERVICING AND EDUCATING AMERICA
A Look at Our Future Society

According to U.S. Labor Department statistics, more than 65.7 million people worked in service industries by 1980. If current employment trends continue as expected, service industries alone should provide work for more than 83.5 million people by 1990.

Lest there be any doubt about the vitality of the service industries as a part of the U.S. economy and as a major employer, estimates indicate they will support more than 88 percent of the American work force by 2000. Of that staggering majority, 44 percent will work in blue-collar jobs, 44 percent in information areas and 12 percent likely will toil in their homes, linked to offices by computers.

Despite its relatively brief history, the U.S. economy has undergone at least three major changes of "heart." What was once an essentially agrarian economy gave way to manufacturing and heavy industry. Now, with smoke chugging, rather than spewing, from the nation's "smokestack" industries, service is king.

Although manufacturing and agriculture remain economic "mainsprings," the service industries increasingly make the economy tick. To put it simply, fewer Americans produce steel, appliances, corn and cars than provide services for workers in those and other industries. The service sector accounts for 84 percent of all new jobs since 1950 and should continue to be the fastest-growing sector of the economy.

New service jobs are expected in many areas, some old, others new. Several factors, including a growing population, more leisure time, shorter work weeks and greater personal income, will spur growth in many traditional service fields.

For example, the country will need about 548,000 security guards, 512,000 police officers and detectives, 103,000 prison officers and 14,000 firefighters by 1990.

As the nation's appetite grows along with its population, about 4,436,000 cooks, 1,700,000 waiters and waitresses and 382,000 bartenders will be needed to satisfy thirsts and hungers.

By 1990, we also should require 565,000 additional hairdressers and cosmetologists, 491,000 housecleaners and servants, 431,000 child care workers, 190,000 butchers and 133,000 bakers.

Although demand in nearly all service job categories is projected to grow, some exceptions exist. Bellhops, for instance, won't experience great demand for their skills and there will be more "downs" than "ups" for elevator operators. Other service industry job categories expected to experience only average, or less than average, growth include: cashier, key punch operator, air traffic controller, postal clerk, mail carrier, telephone operator, flight attendant, truck driver, floral designer, typist and file clerk.

Indicating just how massive the number of service jobs will be, however, is that even "average" growth for typists and cashiers represents 1,023,000 and 1,904,000 jobs respectively by the year 1990.

Along with the traditional service occupations, the continually changing face of U.S. industry should create a variety of new, frequently better-paying jobs requiring more training than their traditional counterparts.

Many of the nation's manufacturing plants will need trained, qualified technicians to service robots, lasers and other high tech manufacturing equipment. Robot service jobs, about 160,000 of them, will be created during the next 10 years.

Hazardous waste technicians, about 300,000, will help monitor and direct clean-up of the nation's land, water and air.

Battery technicians, about 250,000 of them, will maintain the coming generation of batteries or fuel cells used to drive battery-powered houses and cars.

And about 40,000 bartenders must become familiar with computers and cognac as restaurants and bars switch to computerized operations.

In addition to these highly technical jobs, many economists believe the U.S. stands on the verge of creating an entirely new batch of service jobs from those now performed largely on a volunteer basis. Job creation may occur in such diverse areas as reading to children, lobbying for popular causes and teaching the elderly to use computers.

For example, the growth of service industries is so pervasive that just one demographic factor—the increasing number of elderly people living in the U.S.—alone is expected to spawn an entire branch of new services. Consider that in 1975 there were 18.9 retired workers for every 100 active workers. By the year 2030, it's projected, there will be 33.6 retired people for every 100 workers. Where will the new retirees live? What services will they need? Answers to these and other questions should define the boundaries of a new family of service jobs.

Victor Walling, manager of the business futures program at SRI International in California, suggests that these and other new services might include "all the things that are fine, upstanding activities but today lie outside the cash economy."

If the new service jobs are hard to imagine, Walling points out, it was equally difficult a few years ago to foresee that corporations would hire people to monitor environmental impact, guarantee equal employment opportunities and make sure employees receive their proper health care benefits.

EDUCATION AND TEACHERS

But no one is going to benefit at all from more and better jobs unless something is done about how we educate and train people for jobs.

Many studies predict that education fields will produce fewer and fewer jobs—a trend that has already begun. While the overall numbers of teachers may not rise dramatically because of our declining population, nevertheless, we counter that there are good opportunities ahead for those who feel called to teach. This is due to the fact that public attention has turned to education for solutions to the problem of joblessness. Recent media reports about our foreign competitors and their impact on the economy and education are alarming and the American public is clamoring for change. Once-great public and higher educational institutions are no longer working mainly for the good of their own country, for instance, 50 percent of all Ph.D. candidates in the United States are foreigners; 32 percent of all the masters candidates are from other countries, as are 70 percent of all engineering and science advanced degree candidates. Our colleges and universities accept these students because they are the most qualified. Because American students perform more poorly on the SATs, the foreign students outshine them consistently.

Even if U.S. students scored better right now, however, there is another major problem. Currently, potentially competent teachers avoid entering the profession because of low salaries and low esteem—they don't feel wanted, needed or supported by the public they serve. Over the years, teacher education programs have encountered declining enrollments (again, because of low salaries and an oversupply during the baby-boom years and also due to the high status of working in the private sector). To counteract the drop in enrollments, teacher training programs, like so many other professional training programs, lowered their standards for entry. It's a domino effect if there ever was one.

Right now, there are critical teacher shortages in math, science and vocational education areas because these teachers have the skills so highly coveted by business and industry, which are willing to pay comparatively high salaries. Some states are running teachers from other subject areas through intensive math and science prep programs, but this is like putting a butterfly bandage on a gaping open wound.

But the furor raised over the lack of jobs is having a good effect on the educational and training systems, because Americans are taking the time to look at those institutions again. Around the country in the fall of 1983, students and teachers were going back to the classroom with a new sense of purpose and a renewed commitment to the basics.

With the possibility of cooperation between the public and private sectors, teaching may once again be elevated to the professional status it so richly deserves. First, the schools must have a plan, they must know what we expect of them. Are teachers there to teach the basics, expand consciousness, pass on social and cultural niceties, babysit, discipline? In addition to providing funds, equipment and retired managers, scientists, writers, etc., business could teach the schools to plan their business better and react to the marketplace more precisely. And the public tax-paying citizens should be prepared to fork over more money for our schools at all levels whether through shifting funds or increasing revenues. Pinching pennies on the bottom hasn't worked, obviously.

Teachers and vocational trainers must be more demanding. Studies have found that where expectations on the part of a teacher are high, students perform at a higher level and gain a renewed sense of self-esteem. By raising the standards for entry into teacher training programs, we ultimately will have teachers with higher standards and students expecting them. Of course, demanding excellence won't be easy. When Penn State's Joe Paterno and the NCAA decided to require a total of at least 700 on the SAT before accepting college athletes, the wailings from alumni, students and athletics addicts could be heard around the country. Too bad. The ability to think and deduce is more important than the ability to pass, punt and kick except for those few who can and should play games their whole lives. Still, it's tough medicine to swallow for a country which plans its week around Monday, Thursday and Sunday football.

The following list includes more than 50 job categories which are expected to become, or to remain, important segments of service industries. The jobs listed are expected to be created by 1990. Anyone considering a career in those industries would be doing themselves a service by studying the list.

Note that the sheer breadth of the various service industries precludes us from detailing all the jobs here. Additional service industry jobs and their growth potential are detailed in a table near the end of this book.

Job Title	Job Numbers	Starting $	Mid $	Education
Solar Energy Technician	200,000	$13,000	$26,000	2 years college

Installs, repairs and maintains solar energy devices sure to enter the market as solar energy becomes competitive with traditional sources of energy, such as oil, coal and natural gas. New devices include solar "fabric," computer-driven optics which gather and store sunlight, solar "dishes."

| Energy Conservation Technician | 100,000 | $12,000 | $24,000 | 2 years college |

Continuing high prices for heating oil will trigger a demand for experts able to cut heating oil use in homes and factories by using insulation, storm doors and other techniques that keep warm air inside during winter and out during summer.

| Housing Rehabilitation Technician | 500,000 | $14,000 | $24,000 | 2 years vocational |

A doubling of the world population during the next 35 years will lead to mass production of modular housing using new construction techniques and materials. This new breed of repairers will be required to handle the pre-installed heating, electrical, waste disposal, communication and recycling systems.

| Teacher Kindergarten | 243,000 | $15,000 | $25,000 | 4 years college |

Although only average growth is expected, almost a quarter million educational "gatekeepers" will be needed by 1990, especially as the "baby boomers" have their own babies.

| Teacher Elementary School | 1,600,000 | $16,000 | $25,000 | 4 years college |

Again, while about average growth is expected, hundreds of thousands of competent grade school teachers will be required to hold education's front lines.

| Teacher Secondary School | 1,243,000 | $16,000 | $28,000 | 4 years college |

Slower than average growth is projected here, where teachers perform the important task of preparing students for the work world and post-secondary education. In short supply will be math and science teachers.

| Vocational and Educational Counselor | 53,000 | $18,000 | $26,000 | 4 years college |

The nation's education system will need plenty of well-trained "tour guides" to help students plot their individual courses through the continually changing areas of education and employment.

| Rehabili- tation Counselor | 25,000 | $13,000 | $18,000 | 4 years college |

Will assist the mentally, physically and emotionally handicapped to find their niche in school, at work and in everyday life.

| Hazardous Waste Manage- ment Technician | 300,000 | $15,000 | $28,000 | 2 years voca- tional |

Specialist in hazardous waste management will be charged with the collection, transportation, handling, storage and disposal of toxic refuse. The trick in the future will be to avoid the hazardous waste problems we've experienced in the past. Thus, the task of hazardous waste technicians. They don't determine the method—they implement it.

Battery	250,000	$12,000	$18,000	2 years
Technician				voca-
				tional

Will service the coming generation of new high-density batteries or fuel cells used to power homes of the future. The continued high cost of fossil fuels should spur the development of these new power sources.

Electronic	25,000	$16,000	$23,000	2 years
Games				voca-
Repairer				tional

Today's teenage video game enthusiasts may be able to turn their avocation into a futuristic vocation fixing increasingly complex games. Every household with children is expected to have a video game by the year 1990.

Electronic	25,000	$18,000	$25,000	2 years
Casino				voca-
Technician				tional

As more states legalize gambling and casinos and install electronic gaming equipment, a demand for service personnel will result.

Electronic	35,000	$14,000	$20,000	2 years
Mail				voca-
Technician				tional

With electronic mail equipment infiltrating most offices within the next 20 years, many businesses will need in-house technicians to handle service and repairs.

Robot Service-person	160,000	$18,000	$26,000	2 years college

Will maintain, service and repair robots used in a variety of applications, including manufacturing and other industrial procedures. One example of a service that exists *because* of manufacturing, not in place of it.

Nuclear Waste Technician	30,000	$17,000	$23,000	2 years college

Though robots will perform the most hazardous cleanup tasks, a technician will handle the packaging, transportation and disposal of less toxic wasters. As government develops a uniform plan for storing nuclear waste, these jobs should proliferate quickly. These technicians carry out the plans of more trained nuclear experts.

Garbage Disposal Technician	35,000	$16,000	$21,000	2 years vocational

New means of crushing, shredding, compacting and chemically incinerating garbage will require the skills of a disposal technician. With garbage disposal a constant concern on our "shrinking" planet, greater attention must be devoted to the waste disposal and conversion problem.

Computer Bar Technician	40,000	$15,000	$20,000	vocational

As bars and restaurants turn to technology to reduce wasted drinks and food, bartenders of the future will need to be as handy with a computer as they are with a cocktail shaker.

Computer Restaurant Manager	30,000	$17,000	$24,000	vocational

Will order food, check eating trends, schedule staff, and track finances through the use of a computer.

Home Computer Repairer	45,000	$16,500	$22,000	vocational

With the vast majority of homes equipped with personal computers in the future, repairing the machines will become as important a business as building them. Demand estimates for this job could prove very conservative.

Computerized Teaching Assistant	30,000	$14,000	$20,000	4 years college

The proliferation of computers in schools will create the need for teaching assistants trained to help both teachers and students become computer literate.

Electronic Librarian	60,000	$18,000	$24,000	4 years college

Libraries, corporations, colleges, universities, law and medical schools, research laboratories and other institutions will need librarians versed in locating information electronically.

Electronic Information Clerk	50,000	$15,000	$20,000	2 years college

Electronic librarian assistants will handle demanding tasks and process the workload. The electronic information clerk will be the modern equivalent of the reference librarian, except the clerk will have the advantage of a computer to locate "needles" of information in a "haystack" of data.

| Police Computer Technician | 20,000 | $16,000 | $24,000 | 2 years college |

The new forensic expert in the crime lab, the "computer cop" will use computers to trace computer thefts, "regular" thefts, missing persons, etc. Computer theft is among the fastest growing white-collar crimes. In addition, computer system security is a growing area of concern.

| Computer Systems Analyst | 260,000 | $20,000 | $26,000 | 2 years college & vocational |

Analysts use cost accounting, sampling, mathematical models and other methods to design efficient means of processing data. Even computers can be inefficient if not applied properly to a data processing task.

| Computer Programmer | 258,000 | $19,000 | $27,000 | 2 years college |

Although computers are extremely efficient at processing data and performing calculations—so-called "number crunching"—well-trained programmers are necessary to provide the machines with guidance in the form of computer programs. A computer without a program is like a car without a key.

| Holographic Inspector | 200,000 | $18,000 | $20,000 | vocational |

Fiber optics will be used in many manufacturing plants for quality control, scanning and comparing a product with a three-dimensional model inside a computer. The new process creates the need for a different sort of inspector, one who must know computers and fiber optics as well as the product.

| Computer Console and Equipment Operator | 558,000 | $10,000 | $18,000 | vocational |

Will perform the physical functions of entering and receiving data from computers.

| Bank Teller | 531,000 | $8,000 | $12,000 | vocational |

Provides a variety of banking services, which include check cashing, handling deposits and withdrawals, issuing travelers' checks and selling savings bonds.

| Receptionist | 635,000 | $8,000 | $12,000 | vocational |

Despite the high tech tint which colors much of the future, businesses still will need receptionists to greet and offer assistance to visitors and customers as well as perform typing, filing, phone answering and other tasks. This important person typifies the point that high tech high touch must go hand in hand.

| Secretary and Stenographer | 3,940,000 | $9,000 | $12,000 | vocational |

Because secretaries and stenographers perform many tasks vital to an organization's internal workings and communication, their role will continue to be important. They will need to become acquainted with increasingly sophisticated office equipment, however, including speech translating machines, word processors and state-of-the-art telephone gear.

| Social and Recreational Worker | 480,000 | $10,000 | $26,000 | 4 years college |

Social workers will offer aid to people with personal problems, either through counseling or referral to other agencies. Recreation workers will help plan and conduct activities for people with an increasing amount of leisure time available.

| Real Estate Agent and Broker | 582,000 | $13,000 | $29,000 | 4 years college |

Provides an important link between buyers and sellers of property, offering expertise on local housing markets, area zoning and tax regulations and financing.

| Sales Agent, Stocks and Bonds | 67,000 | $11,000 | $50,000 | 4 years college |

Much like real estate agents, these sales agents provide important services for investors looking to buy and sell stocks and bonds.

| Automotive Mechanic | 1,197,000 | $9,000 | $14,000 | vocational |

With people increasingly dependent on automobiles for both business and leisure, plenty of service and repair work will be available. Diesel mechanics particularly are expected to be in great demand.

Radio and Television Mechanic	120,000	$11,000	$19,000	vocational

Look at all the portable radios, tape players, head phones, wrist-watch-size televisions and other appliances, and it's clear repair personnel will be necessary.

Computer Service Technician	93,000	$18,000	$28,000	2 years college

With so many of society's functions increasingly computer reliant, a skilled work force will be required to keep things running smoothly.

Microcomputer Diagnostician	200,000	$20,000	$35,000	2 years college & vocational

Will analyze and test the operations of microcomputers.

Industrial Laser Process Technician	600,000	$30,000	$50,000	vocational

Laser technology will replace many tools found today in mills and foundries. The new equipment will need to be maintained, operated and improved by technicians.

Electric Power Line and Cable Maintenance Mechanic	120,000	$12,000	$18,000	vocational

The widespread and growing use of electricity, along with an occasional heavy wind or ice storm, ensures the need for power line and cable mechanics.

Telephone Installer and Repairer	309,000	$10,000	$12,000	vocational

With the heavy reliance on phone communications during the Information Age, installers and maintenance personnel should have plenty of work.

Cable Television Installer	300,000	$11,000	$13,000	vocational

With pay and subscription television changing the face of television broadcasting and expanding rapidly, installers will be required to "lay the lines."

Home Electronic Interactive Systems Technician	200,000	$15,000	$28,000	vocational

Modern equivalent of TV repairer. He/she will come to your home and repair or adjust your interactive cable. Fifty percent of all homes will have cable by 1987 and will require repair work.

Electrical/ Electronic Engineering Technician	359,000	$12,000	$24,000	vocational

Another home/office repair person. He/she will concentrate on home/office security systems and electronic appliances and equipment used in homes and offices.

Engineering and Science Technician	885,000	$10,000	$12,000	vocational

Takes the engineers' specifications and does the wiring, checking, breadboard soldering, and building.

Materials Utilization Technician	400,000	$15,000	$24,000	4 years college

The future means a diminishing supply of natural materials for production. This technician will develop and suggest substitutes for diminishing or rare materials: ceramics or plastics rather than metals, for example.

Travel Agent	52,000	$10,000	$18,000	vocational or 4 years college

With more time to play, many people will pay travel agents to take the muss and fuss out of planning vacations, making reservations, etc.

Security Guard	548,000	$12,000	$18,000	vocational

Charged with patrolling property to guard against theft, trespassing and vandalism.

Firefighter	14,000	$20,000	$30,000	on the job

Fire is a constant threat in city and countryside alike. Also, arson remains one of the nation's fastest-growing crimes, fanning the need for more firefighters.

Police and Detective	512,000	$15,000	$28,000	4 years college

Unfortunately, crime is expected to be as much a part of the future as it was the past. Computers will streamline and aid in the process, however, and therefore less than average growth is expected.

Correctional Institution Officer	103,000	$12,000	$15,000	2 years college

Called upon to enforce prison rules and maintain order in the nation's prisons and other correctional facilities. Also, these people will be expected to train inmates for jobs, not just warehouse them. Jobs for ex-cons might help lower the return rate.

Food Counter Worker	426,000	$7,000	$14,000	on the job

Will take and deliver orders, issue checks, take payment, and in general cater to the nation's growing appetite for eating out.

Waiter/ Waitress	1,700,000	$7,000	$12,000	on the job

Although growth in this area will be about average, it still will require almost 2 million waiters and waitresses to meet demand by 1990.

Baker	133,000	$9,000	$17,000	apprenticeship and on the job

Although man and woman do not live by bread alone, tens of thousands of bakers will be needed to keep up with demand for pastries, pies, cakes, bread and other bakery delights.

Actuary	20,000	$13,000	$35,000	4 years college

Uses and continually monitors statistics in order to create insurance and pension plans. Math expertise is a must in actuarial work.

Attorney	487,000	$21,000	$60,000	graduate degree

Conducts civil and criminal lawsuits, drafts, legal papers and counsels on laws which touch nearly all segments of society.

Legal Assistant	250,000	$15,000	$20,000	2 years college

Otherwise known as paralegals, these workers often perform research and legwork for a lawyer.

Accountant	1,047,000	$17,000	$25,000	4 years college

Assists companies and individuals in establishing and maintaining their financial recordkeeping procedures.

Bookkeeper	1,904,000	$10,000	$17,000	vocational

Only average growth is predicted, but almost 2 million bookkeepers by the year 1990 will help keep track of the bottom line in businesses and other organizations. Bookkeepers maintain financial records and prepare financial statements.

Advertising Worker	100,000	$10,000	$40,000	4 years college

Assist in planning and implementing advertising campaigns for a variety of products and services.

Energy Auditor	150,000	$12,000	$16,000	vocational

Accountant of energy units rather than monetary units. Measures how much energy is used in homes and buildings and where waste occurs.

Hairdresser/ Cosmetologist	565,000	$7,000	$14,000	vocational

Although this job category should experience only average growth, more than 500,000 hairdressers will be required by 1990 to clip and curl.

Commercial Cook	4,436,000	$7,000	$20,000	vocational

From fry cooks to chefs, from the blue plate special to prime rib, almost 4.5 million cooks must "stand the heat" in kitchens nationwide to satisfy the demand by 1990.

Despite the nearly across-the-board increases projected for service industry jobs during this decade, many economists fear service industries may prove a rather shaky economic base.

The Reagan administration has curtailed hiring in traditionally service-oriented government jobs. At the same time, technology threatens the jobs of many low-level, clerical workers.

Carnegie-Mellon University Economist Steve Miller worries about the "disappearance of the well-paid, blue-collar middle class" and the emergence of a "dual society consisting of low-wage, unskilled service jobs on the one hand and high-wage professional jobs on the other." Miller's concern is not so much that displaced auto workers and steel workers won't have jobs, but that the available jobs will be for busboys, waiters, janitors and clerks.

Columbia University's Eli Ginzburg points out that two-thirds of the jobs created since 1950 can be classified as low-paying, high-turnover and part-time.

"The real danger is that the service industries have no regenerative power," according to Edmund Ayoub, chief economist for the United Steelworkers Union. "If you serve a hamburger at McDonald's, you don't generate any jobs beyond that. If you serve a slab of steel, it has a ripple effect."

Despite those concerns, it would be unrealistic to expect service industries to tread water while the nation looks for complements, or replacements, for its heavy, blue-collar industries.

Besides, contrary to popular belief, service and high technology industries will not completely wipe heavy industry from the U.S. economic map. On the contrary, heavy industries—autos, steel, rubber, textiles, appliances—which incorporate high technology in the manufacturing process should not only survive but also create new jobs.

Consider that when robots replace people in an auto assembly plant, new jobs are created for robot repairers, builders and programmers. Another group will export, market, install and schedule them, adding more thousands of jobs. The same pattern holds for other industries. In order for the service sector to flourish, there must be someone or something to service. Not every service sector employee flips burgers. And as the preceding list of jobs indicated, the salaries many new service jobs will command won't exactly be chopped liver.

For those who gnash their teeth over the evolution of our service-based economy, it should be pointed out that service industries offer one of the best—if not the best—opportunity for an individual with plenty of drive and not much else to start and sustain an entrepreneurial enterprise.

It should also be noted that service industries are basically "clean"—generally free of environmentally harmful side effects and relatively undemanding on the nation's natural resources.

Much of growth in the service industries should bring some good news for the entire economy. Perhaps the prime example is the continuing trend toward working at home. With a computer as his link to the office, nearly any worker who collects and disseminates information can perform without wasting the time and gas necessary to travel to the office.

Some teachers and vocational and educational counselors could conceivably work from their homes. Insurance agents, stock brokers, real estate brokers, travel agents, advertising copywriters and marketing specialists could stay put and produce effectively.

Handicapped people may realize great benefits from the "homework" movements, whether they be students seeking to learn job skills or experienced employees. It's estimated by 2000 more than 500,000 handicapped people will be performing a variety of information service jobs from home.

Self-employed people may eventually become the country's largest work-at-home contingent, including writers, computer programmers, consultants and commercial scholars. And it's projected that by 1990 more than 25 percent of the white collar work force won't set foot in an office.

The information industry giant, IBM, apparently likes this trend. The company expects that as many as one-third of its employees will be working at home by 1990.

For those already employed in the service industries, or those who might fill one of the millions of service jobs created in the coming years, the work-at-home movement is just one more reason to "expect there will be a job in your future."

3

HEALTH
AND HEALTH-RELATED
JOBS

New Trends

Imagine an industry that is virtually recession proof, boasts a potential customer base numbering in the billions and owns a record for cranking out amazing advances and astounding achievements on nearly a daily basis.

Imagine a field that offers many high-paying jobs and which will likely require more than 3 million new, well-trained, dedicated professionals during the next 20 years.

And imagine work which involves nothing more vital than curing diseases, mending handicaps, alleviating suffering and enhancing both the longevity and quality of life for all people.

Sound like a winner? Then open your mouth and say "Ahhh," because the industry in question is one we lump under the increasingly expanding umbrella known as medicine and health.

Perhaps more than any other field, the medical and health industry melds man, machines and imagination in an industry that routinely reports new accomplishments and never lacks for new challenges. Although they already boast an impressive track record, medical professionals face fresh trials as they round each turn.

Since the 20th century began, the average lifespan of the people in the U.S. has increased from 48 to 72 years. In 1940, infection caused 25 percent of all deaths. The discovery of penicillin and its descendant antibiotics cut that figure to 3 percent. Similar landmark medical achievements in the years to come are expected to extend the average lifespan even further. So much so, in fact, that a child born today should live to be 83 years old—10 years more than its parents, 20 more than its grandparents and 30 more than its great-grandparents.

Medical "engineers" now craft artificial hearts and have developed artificial blood. Surgical specialists have made the heart transplant a procedure that now borders on routine. Brains are explored, limbs are reattached and cancer cells are bombed with radiation and deluged with chemotherapy in an effort to find a winning combination.

These advances in the technical aspects of medicine have not been without their parallels in what might be called "good, old-fashioned healthy living." "Wellness," a new-fangled term for the ancient idea of "an ounce of prevention," encompasses a trend that has people living and working more healthfully, eating better and exercising with a vengeance. A by-product of the health craze has been a small-business boom in health-food stores, exercise clubs, books and records and sports fashions.

Medical advances and a greater attention to healthy lifestyles, in turn, contribute to an increasing average lifespan, leaving a larger and older population anxiously anticipating the next medical marvel. The U.S. Census Bureau reports that the number of Americans 65 years of age and older will more than double—to more than 66 million people—during the next 50 years. During the same period, the number of people beyond 85 years of age should nearly triple. Imagine how these improvements will boost the over-100 population, now pegged at 32,000.

What all of these factors mean for the field of medicine and health is continued growth, myriad changes and plenty of jobs, some not even imagined only a few years ago.

As *U.S. News & World Report* put it, the spectacular growth projected in the medical field is expected, indeed caused, because "medicine dares to dream the impossible."

Among the "impossible" tasks which lie ahead is the eventual prevention and treatment of most genetic diseases, such as sickle cell anemia and muscular dystrophy. Other "impossibilities" include discovering the basic causes of cancer and heart disease. What about such "impossible" challenges as finding new drugs that dissolve gall and kidney stones? Finding new treatments for hypertension, high blood pressure and arteriosclerosis? Or such improbable creations as artificial blood vessels, skin, knees, hips, fingers, hands, arms, ears, tongues, kidneys and livers?

Impossible? Don't bet on it. "The real breakthrough will come in the 21st century," according to the University of Utah's Dr. Steven Jacobson. "That's when we'll be able to regenerate limbs, not just make artificial replacements."

And while you're at it, don't bet against most of the other "impossibilities" mentioned above. Consider gene splicing, once considered just another member of the medical "impossible dream" scrap heap. Researchers in Sweden already are exploring using the gene-splicing technique to manufacture what they call the Human Growth Hormone (HGH), a hormone produced in the pituitary gland which regulates a person's growth. The fruits of their experiments could eventually be used to help dwarfs attain "normal" height and otherwise alter the highs and lows of human growth patterns.

Another area in which gene splicing is almost certain to play an important role is in the production of interferon, a protein the human body produces to combat viral infections. Scientists suspect interferon may be a vital weapon in the fight against cancer, because it tends to block viruses from hopping from one cell to another. Because the body produces interferon in minute amounts, it is difficult to draw the protein directly from humans. But by splicing interferon-producing cells onto a bacteria that divides and reproduces itself rapidly, a cellular "factory" of interferon-producing organisms can be created.

Gene splicing is just one potentially fertile patch in the large field of medical research, a field where scientists, researchers and medical specialists continually dig for new answers. The implications gene splicing holds for battling disease are obvious, and staggering. And at the same time, that single medical endeavor promises to trigger a sluice of jobs in the areas of research, testing, production and delivery of the final products.

Countless physicists, chemists, biologists, lab technicians, engineering and other trained professionals are required to take such a concept from the medical drawing board to hospitals and clinics throughout the world. By 1990, for example, the U.S. is expected to need as many as 150,000 genetic engineers to spearhead research projects in gene splicing and other genetic fields.

In addition, at least 110,000 genetic engineering technicians will likely be needed to oversee the thousands of gene "factories" expected to spring up across the country. As more genetically engineered compounds become available, more workers will likely be needed to test, store and distribute the products. Genetically engineered material is also expected to open a new field of patent law, calling for specially trained lawyers and paralegal assistants.

The medical research domain is filled with similar research endeavors, projects that hold the promise of better health for all and exciting employment opportunities for many.

Pharmaceutical companies, for example, are already making their reservations on the U.S. space shuttle, where they hope to study the feasibility of manufacturing serums and vaccines amid the weightless environment of space. If the experiments prove successful, one company, Johnson & Johnson, plans to place a vaccine-manufacturing robot satellite in space.

Some drug companies are experimenting with vaccine patches, which are attached to the skin and secrete drugs into the body. Other scientists are exploring the possibility of concocting vaccines to prevent such tenacious diseases as tuberculosis and cancer.

Lasers already aid surgeons in their precise and demanding work. The laser is expected to play an especially important role in the areas of eye, nose, ear and throat surgery.

And experiments are now underway to determine whether damaged brain cells and spines—once thought beyond repair—can be rejuvenated. In the pursuit of these and other medical "impossibilities," jobs are certain to be a by-product.

Jobs will also be created in the design, manufacture, repair and operation of a variety of new medical equipment and machines. About 50,000 biomedical engineers will be required by 1990 to manufacture an arsenal of new electronic machinery for diagnosis and treatment of disease. Another 90,000 bioelectronic technicians will be needed to maintain and repair those devices. Two examples of recently created medical hardware are the computer axial tomography (CAT) and the positron emission transaxial tomography (PETT) scanners. The machines combine X-ray capability with computer technology to produce cross-sectional views of the body. We'll need about 45,000 CAT scan technicians and about 165,000 PETT scan technicians to operate the machinery by 1990.

We can also add bionics to the long and continually growing list of medical specialties which are likely to create jobs. For instance, about 110,000 bionic technicians will be needed to manufacture the artificial hands, fingers, legs and knees mentioned earlier. In addition, 40,000 orthotists will be required to help people ensure their artificial appendages fit properly.

There is little doubt that future medical innovations—and the jobs they will create—will be numerous. What cannot be predicted, however, are those medical advances and related jobs which lie just beyond what some see as today's medical "impossibilities."

It should be noted that traditional health care careers will not be without growth. About 550,000 practical nurses, for example, will be needed by 1990. Also, more than 1.3 million registered nurses will be required to provide the "nuts and bolts" of health care. We'll also need to add about 141,000 pharmacists, who will be hard-pressed to keep abreast of the latest drugs.

As stated earlier, increasingly sophisticated health care will greatly increase the average person's lifespan and produce an older U.S. population. Luckily, because living longer isn't tantamount to living better, the health industries will adapt to this "graying" population.

Doctors at the University of Liege in Belgium are experimenting with a human hormone, vasopressin, which may play an important role in enhancing memory and retarding senility. Already, a man who spent 15 days in a coma after an automobile accident, and recalled nothing after the crash, described all the details after seven days of vasopressin treatments. Another man, who played chess when he was young but later forgot how, is now playing and beating younger players after receiving treatment.

Estimates reveal that by 2000 the growing number of elderly people will spawn the creation of a million new jobs. It's projected, for example, that by 1990 more than 450,000 people will be needed to fill the yet-to-be-created job of geriatric social worker. Old people face a variety of problems: decreased mobility, limited income, debilitating diseases, the loss of loved ones, alienation from society. Geriatric social workers will be called upon to provide a variety of outreach programs, training, physical and emotional therapy, transportation and housing assistance and companionship. Geriatric social technicians, about 300,000 of them, will be employed to help hard-of-hearing and visually handicapped old people work with computers and new hearing and visual aids.

Clearly, the future of medicine and the health-related fields is filled with mind-rattling possibilities for both the enhancement of health and the employment of people. If all this talk of artificial organs, gene splicing and bionics sounds a bit too much like the plot for a late-night rerun of "The Six Million Dollar Man," think again.

Many of the ideas discussed above are being explored and tested now. And many medical professionals and aspiring health care specialists already are anticipating the hundreds of thousands of jobs that must be filled if medical speculation and experimentation are ever to become reality.

Training and education for many traditional jobs in the medical field are available at thousands of colleges, universities, junior colleges and vocational facilities scattered liberally across the country. Those considering careers in more specialized areas—those requiring graduate work or relatively new training techniques—may need to search farther afield to find the school or training program right for them. And for some of the jobs mentioned in this chapter, the educational requirements only now are being defined.

What follows is a list of more than 30 job categories— some new, many not—which are expected to experience moderate to rapid employment growth by 1990. Some of the job titles and descriptions may be difficult to pronounce, much less visualize.

But take the time and try. Because, historically, medicine and health is a field limited only by the imagination and brimming with innumerable job possibilities. Here are just a few.

Job Title	Job Numbers	Starting $	Mid $	Education
Radiologic Technologist	65,000	$10,000	$18,000	2 years college

An X-ray technician with more skills and duties, this person will conduct X-ray examinations, understand body mechanics, safety procedures and new, faster, safer machines coming to market. The biggest change will be in processing the X-ray film so computers can enhance it for doctors to study.

Radiation Therapy Technologist	100,000	$10,500	$17,000	2 years vocational

Will operate new radiation machines to treat cancer patients. Must be knowledgeable with different types of machines, will have to be retrained to handle newer machines. Must have full understanding of doses for each patient and be aware that focusing the radiation on a single body position is a life and death matter. As new radiation treatments are created, the demand for this job will grow rapidly.

Nuclear Medical Technologist	75,000	$18,000	$29,000	2–4 years college

Will help diagnose diseases using radioscope tracers and treat diseases using a growing array of radioactive medicines. As isotopes are absorbed in soft body tissues and muscle, a diagnostician observes how damaged and diseased tissue/muscle responds. Must understand how computers will improve video displays of isotope flow and response as it moves through the body. With advanced understanding of radiomedicine and its enhancement by computerized display, a substantial increase in demand for this skill lies ahead. Even to fill current needs, 600 nuclear technologists must be trained each year for the next 5 years.

| Diagnostic Sonographer | 70,000 | $11,000 | $25,000 | 2 years college |

Will use new sonic probes coming to market, off-spring of once-classified devices used by Navy to detect submarines and underwater mines. X-ray technicians could be trained for this job or sonar specialists coming out of Navy who studied physics, anatomy and physiology in college. Sonic probes will be safer in some cases than X-rays, particularly in obstetrics, gynecology and ophthamology.

| Respiratory Therapist | 50,000 | $11,000 | $22,000 | 2 years college |

Works in and out of operating room using new, computerized methods of providing breathing assistance for patients with heart and lung conditions. Instructs patients in breathing exercises and use of respiratory aids.

| Respiratory Technician | 50,000 | $10,000 | $18,000 | 1 year training |

Works mostly in operating room administering oxygen and assisting anesthesiologist in administration of anesthetic gases like ether and nitrous oxide. Knows how to use artificial airways, ventilators, etc., to resuscitate patients who stop breathing. While this is not a new job, its description and the number needed for many more will change as respiratory equipment changes over the next 20 years.

| Cardiopulmonary Specialist | 35,000 | $13,000 | $20,000 | 2 years training |

Diagnoses heart and lung ailments using newer invasive (chemical dyes, tubes) and non-invasive (ultrasound, echocardiograms) techniques.

| Cardiopul-
monary
Technician | 30,000 | $9,500 | $20,000 | 1 year
training |

Assists in operating room during open heart surgery or where removal of lung is required. Operates machinery that assists heartbeat. With experience and more training, this person becomes a Cardiopulmonary Specialist.

| Electroen-
cephalo-
gram
Technolo-
gist (EEG) | 85,000 | $11,000 | $18,000 | 1 year
training |

Gives electroencephalograms, using computers to help look for brain disorders or disorders that show up on EEG relating to metabolic change, blood chemistry change, shortage of oxygen in brain, etc. Big change here is knowing the link between EEG and computers.

| Dialysis
Technician | 30,000 | $14,000 | $23,000 | 2 years
training |

Provides the technical support for dialysis care team, whose numbers grow daily as better and cheaper kidney machines make dialysis available to more kidney disease victims. Also, maintains and repairs the machinery. The auto mechanic of the dialysis team.

| Perfusionist | 40,000 | $12,000 | $20,000 | 2 years
college |

Operates the newest heart-lung machines to maintain oxygen circulation throughout body during open-heart surgery.

| Bioelectronic
Technician | 90,000 | $11,000 | $19,000 | 2 years
college |

Maintains and repairs the mounting (seemingly endless) number of new electronic biomedical machines used in diagnosis, treatment and surgery. Has to be a good electronic technician and understand anatomy and physiology.

Biomedical Engineer	50,000	$20,000	$35,000	4 years college and/or graduate school

Designs and develops new electronic machinery to diagnose and treat disease. This field has opportunities that are as unlimited as they are unpredictable. Look for a Nobel Prize winner to come out of this field.

Genetic Engineering Technician	250,000	$20,000	$30,000	4 years college

While production in a "biotech" plant takes place inside the cells of microorganisms that have been genetically altered, there will be so many of these "gene machines" in the future—making everything from insulin to interferon to genetically altered corn seeds to new fertilizer—that we predict this to be one of the technician jobs of the future. Typical biotech plants will have only 150 technicians, but there will be thousands of biotech plants built from Long Island to Los Angeles in the next 20 years.

Bionic Technician	110,000	$21,000	$32,000	4 years college

The "bionic" equal of the "genetic" technician listed above, this person will be the mechanic who manufactures electronically controlled artificial limbs and organs that will perform almost as well as real limbs and organs. While some technicians will make the appendage or organ, others will install its electronic controls. Professionals who establish reputations in these fields will move rapidly into 6-figure earnings levels.

Dental Laboratory Technician	53,000	$17,000	$30,000	vocational training

As the nation's population ages, so will its teeth. Lab technicians make artificial dentures, teeth, crowns, bridges and other dental work prescribed by dentists.

Medical Laboratory Technician	205,000	$12,000	$21,000	2 years college

Performs a variety of tests—including chemical, immunological, microbiological and hematological exams—under the direction of a medical technologist.

Physician Assistant	10,000	$18,000	$22,000	4 years college

Provides a variety of services—including interviewing patients and performing physical exams—under the direct supervision of medical and osteopathic doctors.

Midwife	15,000	$10,000	$20,000	apprentice training

As medical teams travel to homes, the midwife's role becomes more popular again. Will conduct at-home delivery for pregnant women.

Audiologist		$15,000	$27,000	4–6 years college

Diagnoses and treats people with hearing problems. May also prescribe specialized equipment, such as hearing aids, for the hearing impaired.

Paramedic	400,000	$16,000	$29,000	4 years college

Previous "paramedics" needed no college education, just battlefield experience in Vietnam. But the shortage of doctors and nurses, plus the proliferation of new medical equipment, intensive care units, longer treatment of serious disease and the emergence of mobile emergency medical teams, means paramedics must be college graduates with the same premedical degrees medical students need to enter medical schools. Paramedics, while linked by radio to hospital personnel, provide emergency medical treatment on the scene.

Geriatric Service Worker	700,000	$15,000	$22,000	2 years college

By the year 2000, the birthrate of Americans will merely equal the "replacement rate." So many elderly will need mental, physical and social care that there will have to be a social worker trained specifically in care for the elderly.

Computer Axial Tomography Technician	45,000	$13,000	$20,400	2 years college

Though more than a decade has passed since development of the CAT Scanner, which blends X-rays with computer technology to give cross-sectional views of the body, the job of running the machinery has since been the doctor's. No longer. With too many machines getting too much use and not enough doctors to manage them all, it has now become a technician's job.

Positron Emission Transaxial Tomography (PETT) Technician	165,000	$14,500	$17,500	2 years college

PETT scanners, the newest and most direct descendants of the CAT scanner, are now being used to diagnose brain disorders. Again, doctors once had sole rights to this machine. Again, there are too many machines and too few doctors.

Diagnostician for Handicapped Persons	80,000	$13,400	$17,000	2 years college

Will use computers to help diagnose the extent of a handicapped victim's injuries, enabling therapists to use those same computers to devise the best means of therapy to rehabilitate the patient.

Therapist for Handicapped Persons	120,000	$13,700	$18,500	2 years college

New treatments to rehabilitate the severely handicapped plus better job opportunities for handicapped people when they are rehabilitated means this job is a new one. New methods of therapy alone make it a job that will be in large demand for years to come.

Geriatric Social Technician	300,000	$12,500	$17,500	2 years college

Will use computers and new hearing devices, as well as new Braille machines, to assist deaf and blind aged to hear others speak, read books and enjoy television.

Paraveterinarian	30,000	$11,000	$16,000	2 years college

So many veterinarians are at work in America today they can no longer do the job alone. A nurse they don't need. A paravet with an understanding and fondness for animals they need.

| Computer Speech Pathologist | 40,000 | $19,000 | $25,000 | 4 years college |

Uses computerized aids to diagnose and treat people with speech impediment and language difficulties. We've had speech pathologists for many years. The computer will place more demands on, and offer more opportunities for, these professionals.

| Psychiatric Chemo-therapist | 35,000 | $21,000 | $34,000 | 4 years college |

Will require a degree in biochemistry. Because there will be so many new treatments for mental and psychiatric disorders during the next 20 years, the doctor will need to call on the services of this specialist to treat the disorder.

| Orthotist | 40,000 | $14,000 | $16,500 | 2 years training |

Fits artificial limbs and braces to help patients cope with deformities and amputations. Making an artificial limb is only half the task. Getting it to fit is an important and ongoing part of the process.

| Computer Dietetic Specialist | 30,000 | $12,500 | $17,000 | 2 years training |

Uses the computer to devise special diets for the ill and those recovering from surgery. Just one more new job made available through computers.

| Genetic Engineer | 150,000 | $23,000 | $38,000 | graduate school |

Don't let the title "engineer" mislead you. This professional won't be working with girders and gears. Instead, genetic engineers will use the basic building blocks of human life as their raw materials. Through manipulation of the human genetic code, they will likely explore gene splicing, limb regeneration and other medical quandaries.

Dental Hygienist	36,000	$11,000	$14,000	4 years college

Performs much of the groundwork for dentists, including taking x-rays of a patient's teeth, cleaning teeth, obtaining medical and dental histories, assisting the dentist and instructing the patient on proper medical care.

Pharmacist	141,000	$21,000	$24,000	4 years college

Provides patients with the drugs and medicine prescribed by doctors. With the likelihood that many new medicines will hit the market in coming years, pharmacists will be challenged to stay abreast of the most recent developments in pharmaceutical medicine.

Registered Nurse	1,302,000	$14,000	$20,000	4 years college

The list of tasks performed by registered nurses in hospitals, clinics, nursing homes and other facilities across the country is too long to completely detail here. In general, RNs are charged with observing and recording patient symptoms, administering medication and providing many other health care tasks. Because nurses are in demand nearly everywhere, nursing often permits an individual to move freely without fear of not finding work.

Licensed Practical Nurse	550,000	$9,000	$12,000	2 years college

LPNs provide much of the bedside care patients require. LPNs receive training that's more technical than the broader medical training demanded of registered nurses. LPNs often take temperature and blood pressure readings, assist patients with their personal hygiene and assist physicians in examining patients.

Clearly the field of medicine and health will be filled with remarkable achievements, tremendous growth and a multitude of job opportunities for years to come.

But these thousands of new jobs—in areas ranging from paramedicine to biotechnology, genetic engineering to gerontology—will not be attained without proper and rigorous training.

In fact, the new generation of medical professionals will need to be better trained, more educated and more highly skilled than any which has gone before it. Although the jobs may be rewarding in both human and monetary terms, they may also be among the most demanding in any industry.

Along with the medical advances will come difficult moral and ethical questions. The new medical professionals may not only have to be supremely educated, but also extremely sensitive to the questions and problems posed by a continuing stream of medical "miracles." These are national issues and training is certain to address them.

According to the *U.S. News and World Report,* spending on health care in the U.S. will climb from the current 10 percent of the Gross National Product to 15 percent by 2000 and 20 percent by 2033. Who should have access to the latest in modern medical techniques, who can afford the latest in medical treatment and where the happy medium lies may prove difficult and persistent questions.

"We will increasingly face tough decisions about who will receive certain lifesaving but expensive equipment," said Dr. Howard Hiatt, dean of Harvard's School of Public

Health. "We must find ways of making the wisest decisions."

At the same time, for those seeking a meaningful job in an industry with almost limitless potential for growth, choosing a career in the field of medicine and health would seem a wise decision.

4

ENGINEERING IN THE FUTURE

The Expanding Technology

Although the future brims with promises of technological advances that should radically alter the way we live and work, these historic changes won't happen accidentally.

Robots don't make themselves—at least not yet. It'll take more than wishful thinking to manufacture artificial limbs, replacement organs and a variety of medical implants and treatment devices. And although teletext technology heralds a new era in handling and distributing goods, services and information, it will take more than a flip of a switch or the touch of a button to start the process.

The U.S. will require the services of an army of highly trained, extremely imaginative and resourceful engineers and scientific specialists to coax many technological advances off the futuristic drawing boards into reality.

By the year 1990, this country will need hundreds of thousands of engineers in virtually all the field's specialty areas. For instance, more than 350,000 additional electrical and electronic engineers will be in demand in order to spearhead the skyrocketing computer, electronics and semiconductor revolution. As many as 180,000 civil engineers will be called upon to help salvage—and in some cases resurrect—the nation's crumbling infrastructure of roads, bridges, water and sewer systems and the many other "building blocks" of an industrialized nation. As many as a half-million robotics engineers are expected to improve productivity by introducing robots into manufacturing, farming, construction and many other sectors. Demand for engineers also will be great in the aerospace, petroleum, mining, nuclear power and health-related industries. And similar job growth should occur in chemistry, physics, geophysics and architecture, where experts will be charged with tasks ranging from developing new, strong synthetic materials to designing portable, energy-efficient housing.

It's no surprise that in a country betting on technological advances to grow its economy, engineers and scientists will be in great demand and can expect to command attractive salaries. What is surprising—and troubling—is that the same country is seen by many as poorly equipped to adequately train and educate qualified candidates for an avalanche of new and demanding jobs.

Estimates indicate that U.S. industries already face a 10 to 20 percent annual shortfall of well-qualified engineering school graduates. That shortage balloons to more than 50 percent in computer-related fields. U.S. engineering schools graduate only 50,000 engineers of *all* types each year, and a large number of those are foreigners. Also, each year we lose many experienced engineers because of burnout, boredom or lack of updated skills.

For example, in 1982 a study conducted for former California Governor Jerry Brown revealed that while the state's electronics companies will create 62,000 jobs during the next 5 years, California's colleges and universities are expected to produce only 14,000 engineers—less than one-fifth the demand—during the same 5 years.

Along with the engineer shortage, there's another related problem. The nation's educational system seems to be coming up short in providing math and science instruction, the nuts and bolts of an engineering education. It's estimated that only one-third of the nation's secondary schools provide enough math and science courses to qualify their students for entrance at accredited engineering schools. (And this indicates a high demand for math and science teachers.) At that same time, test scores for students taking the available math and science courses steadily decline.

Many 4-year engineering students are shunning graduate school in favor of high-paying jobs in private industry. Nearly half of the engineering graduate students enrolled in U.S. colleges and universities are from foreign countries.

W. L. Somervell, Jr., director of a Colorado State University program called Engineering Renewal and Growth, summarized the problem by noting that "whereas the United States is competing with other industrialized nations for the benefit of technology, our schools are turning out few of the front runners needed to win the contest."

Thomas A. Vanderslice, president of CTE Corp., is similarly apprehensive about the decline of engineers, saying, "I'm scared to death about the [small] number of technical people that are going to be available."

The problems created by the shortage and lagging education in math and science are not lost on officials in private industry, government and education. Schools have a difficult time attracting engineering, science and math instructors. Unfortunately for academe, the choice between $12,000 per year teaching and more than $20,000 per year working in private industry often proves to be no choice at all. Qualified candidates also are lured by the private sector's modern research facilities and equipment. Thus, about 2,000 engineering teaching positions—about 10 percent of the nation's total—go unfilled.

Industry, meanwhile, finds itself strapped without qualified scientists and engineers to solve the riddles of technological progression. William Howard, a vice president with Motorola, said, "The shortage has slowed down our progress, slowed down our development of new prices and slowed down our ability to do maintenance. The net effect is to put things on hold or do them more slowly until we can recruit the talent."

Finally, government officials watch as U.S. colleges and universities produce highly educated engineers for foreign countries while this nation's industries lose technological ground to foreign competitors.

Just as officials in education, government and private industry bear witness to the problems posed by an engineering decline, they also may hold the answers. Innovative and extensive cooperation among industry, education and government will be required to bolster the country's engineer pool to meet the coming demand.

One such program is the "Center for Excellence in Engineering" at Arizona State University. There, the state government, the university and private companies created a $32 million program to increase engineering teacher salaries while boosting the university's engineering faculty by about 60 teachers. Another exercise in enlightened self-interest has companies like Bechtel, Shell Oil, Xerox, Control Data and International Business Machines donating technical experts to work with students in selected schools.

Recent rumblings from Washington indicate the federal government is about ready to do its part to halt the slide in engineering. Proposed legislation would once again institute tax incentives for research and development. The Reagan administration has proposed spending $50 million to train math and science teachers for 4 years. The Democrat-controlled House of Representatives, not to be outdone, approved a bill in March 1983 calling for spending $425 million on math and science instruction.

Luckily, the trend toward forsaking math and science already has begun to reverse itself—prodded by concerned parents, *Time* magazine reports that during the past 3 years more than half of the nation's 16,000 school districts boosted the credits required in subjects such as English, science and mathematics. Another 38 percent are expected to follow suit by 1985.

Regardless of how we mend the process of training engineers and scientists, it would be to the nation's advantage to do so—and quickly. As noted earlier, job projections in nearly all engineering fields and many scientific disciplines call for fast growth. The challenges facing those technical experts will be as numerous and complex as any in our history. Genetic engineering, artificial intelligence, seeing, hearing and thinking computers, robotics, nuclear power, telecommunication, the choices are nearly endless.

Even the tools engineers and scientists use to design computers, robots and artificial organs are new and complex. Computer-aided design (CAD) rapidly is replacing the comfortable, old-fashioned drawing board. An engineer can use CAD to design a product on a computer screen—adding, deleting, shaping, testing—without the time and hassle of drawing, redrawing, building prototypes, testing and then perhaps starting the process over from scratch. And computer-aided manufacturing (CAM) allows an engineer to store parts in a computer rather than a warehouse. The parts can then be manufactured and altered as needed. Say hello to CAM, bid adios to wasteful inventory expenses.

A Michigan company, Koltanbar Engineering, estimates that CAD/CAM allows its engineers to draw in a day what once took 120 hours, to complete in about 80 weeks a project that formerly required more than 4 years.

The training required for many engineering specialties is similar in many respects. What differs is the problems each engineer encounters once on the job. Whether it's a mechanical engineer designing a robot arm or a bionic engineer building a human limb, many of the principles are similar, only the applications differ.

High school students anticipating a career in engineering should tend to their "Ps and Qs" in all subjects, especially science and math.

Those considering an engineering college, university or graduate school can scan the appendix near the back of this book to find the leading universities in the respective engineering specialties. By balancing cost, location and academic reputation, they should be able to locate a school to fit their needs.

Furthermore, engineers should remember that the doors to upper management are not closed to them because they are technocrats. In fact, many business observers contend that engineers make the best CEOs because they understand the need for research and development. This gives them a long-term view rather than the cold-hearted "bottom line" viewpoint of the MBA-trained executive. Some of the most successful, humane U.S. companies grew under the tutelage of an "engineering type."

The following list includes several job categories in the engineering and science fields and the number of jobs that should be available by 1990. These and many other related jobs should be available as we move into the technologically complex years ahead. The biggest challenge we face may not be creating these jobs, but filling them.

Job Title	Job Numbers	Starting $	Mid $	Education
Electrical or Electronic Engineer	357,000	$22,000	$33,000	4 years college

Directs the building and operation of a variety of electronic and electrical devices. Specialties include communications, electronics, power distribution, integrated circuits, computers, etc. The largest branch of engineering.

Job Title	Job Numbers	Starting $	Mid $	Education
Civil Engineer	180,000	$20,000	$27,000	4 years college

Oversees the design and construction of roads, bridges, tunnels, water and sewer systems and buildings. With the nation's decaying infrastructure of increasing concern, many jobs should be available in specialties such as structural, hydraulic, highway and transportation engineering.

Mechanical Engineer	237,000	$20,000	$28,000	4 years college

The "power broker" of the engineering field. Designs, builds and services power-generating engines (steam engines, jet engines, gas turbines, rocket engines) and machines (jets, appliances, drills, presses) which use those engines to perform work. Positions should be available in areas ranging from teaching to testing.

Chemical Engineer	55,000	$22,000	$33,000	4 years college

Although only average growth is expected until 1990, thousands of jobs still will be available in areas which include chemical research and production, synthetic fuels and anti-pollution research.

Industrial Engineer	245,000	$22,000	$30,000	4 years college

Juggles the basic components of manufacturing to determine the most efficient use of people, materials and tools. Efficiency is the bottom line here.

Biomedical Engineer	4,000	$18,000	$28,000	graduate school

Will oversee the design and operation of electronic communication video and sound equipment for the coming field of teletext communication—shopping by video screen and ordering by phone.

Aerospace Engineer	90,000	$22,000	$30,000	4 years college

Participates in all facets of aircraft, missile and space vehicle production, including design, construction and testing. Government support—or lack thereof—will have a tremendous impact on this engineering field.

| Agricultural Engineer | 17,500 | $20,000 | $30,000 | 4 years college |

The "down-on-the-farm" counterpart of the aerospace engineer, agricultural engineers design and test equipment used in the production and processing of farm products. Computers, lasers and other high tech machinery are expected to be as common on farms as in factories during the coming years.

| Metallurgical Engineer | 25,000 | $20,000 | $30,000 | 4 years college |

Researches and creates new varieties of metals designed to meet a variety of specific needs, including strength, heat resistance, malleability, etc.

| Petroleum Engineer | 25,000 | $24,000 | $35,000 | 4 years college |

Concerned with locating, drilling and refining petroleum and natural gas. As oil becomes increasingly scarce, new recovery methods will provide challenges, as will other energy sources, such as oil shale and tar sands.

| Mining Engineer | 10,000 | $21,000 | $32,000 | 4 years college |

Develops plans for mining operations, including both open pit and underground sites. Concerned with providing adequate power supplies, water, lighting, ventilation, transportation and communication.

| Nuclear Engineer | 12,000–25,000 | $21,000 | $30,000 | 4 years college |

Participates in the design, construction and operation of nuclear power plants. Also designs and oversees systems for handling nuclear waste. Government policy will have much to do with future growth prospects in this area.

Chemist	128,000	$20,000	$35,000	4 years college

Although only average growth is expected for this job category, nearly every facet of our lives is touched by the results of chemical research—everything from the food we eat to the clothes we wear.

Physicist	44,000	$15,000	$22,000	4 years college

Teaching, research and testing duties will require the skills of thousands of physicists—the people who explain the mechanical workings of our universe.

Geophysicist	12,000	$20,000	$28,000	4 years college

Conducts research into oil and mineral deposits and monitors earthquake activity with the help of complex electronic equipment. Despite projections of only average growth, many geophysicists will find work with oil and gas companies. A similar outlook is predicted for geologists, where 34,000 new jobs are expected by 1990.

Architect	79,000	$14,000	$40,000	4 years college

Designs buildings, parking ramps and landscape layouts with attention to safety, energy efficiency, cost efficiency and aesthetics.

It would be dangerous and misleading to suggest that the responsibility of keeping our country's technological "house" in order rests solely with educators and future engineers and scientists. The need for greater awareness and training in science, math and technology is one none of us can ignore.

Walk into a school computer lab, read newspapers and magazines, scan the book shelves. You'll find that high technology is not only on the way, it's here and it's almost everywhere. People will no longer be able to dismiss computers with a frown, a wave of the hand and a muttered, "I'll never understand those darn things. I don't want anything to do with them." When a computer balances your checkbook, runs the house lights and heating system, governs your car, helps you shop and sits squarely in the middle of your desk at work, it's pretty tough to ignore. We'll all need a greater understanding of technology in order to function and live fully. People either will learn to get along in the new electronic age or be continually frustrated by it.

Colorado State University's Somervell said, "In an era of technological explosions, at a time when scientific knowledge has increased more in the last 40 years than in all prior recorded history and the technological half-life of an engineer is less than five years, the majority of America's citizens lack the understanding and skills necessary to participate fully in the technological world in which we live and work."

In order to prevent "technological illiteracy" from running rampant, individuals must take responsibility for keeping themselves abreast of technology. It shouldn't be too difficult. It'll be in all the papers.

Industry, too, can play its part by paying as much attention to retraining employees as they do to upgrading robots and incorporating new technologies.

And education can help considerably by rededicating its efforts in the subjects of math and science. One school, the Rochester Institute of Technology in Rochester, New York, is already doing its part. In 1982, R.I.T. became the first U.S. school to offer a bachelor's degree in microelectronic engineering. Even more importantly, all R.I.T. graduates—regardless of their major field of study—must learn the operations of a computer.

By 1985, it's projected that at least 10 percent of all engineering schools will require students to own a personal computer as a prerequisite for acceptance. Although the demand for student-owned hardware may sound a bit excessive, graduates of those schools will likely recoup the expense many times over in the higher salaries they'll command for their computer expertise.

Not surprisingly, business and education can be of great assistance to one another in the quest for improved math, science and computer skills among students. Businesses can offer technical experts and equipment to school. Education—in the process of teaching and learning—can provide business with software, research and employable, highly trained graduates. Such "you scratch my back, I'll scratch yours" relationships already exist in the Silicon Valley near Stanford University in California, in a belt of high technology businesses near the Massachusetts Institute of Technology in Boston, and in a batch of bionics enterprises near the University of Utah.

As we pointed out earlier, the jobs should be there. The big task will be to fill them with educated, qualified people.

5

COMMUNICATIONS AND THE ARTS

The New Vision of the Information Age

Traditionally, parents have winced, argued and finally clutched their pocketbooks in dread after children announced plans to pursue acting, music, writing, or art.

Employment growth in these communicative and creative professions, historically, has been about as weak as the *Mona Lisa's* smile. Although it would be nice to report a change in that employment trend during the remainder of this decade, in most cases it simply won't happen. Actors, musicians, and artists can expect agony in strong doses as they struggle toward the success only a few attain. The road to Broadway and artistic fame remains littered with fractured dreams. For every star embedded in a Hollywood sidewalk, a galaxy of hopes glimmered and died.

Luckily for nervous parents and future communicators, employment prospects in the area of communication and entertainment are not universally dismal. After all, we're in the midst of what's come to be called "The Information Age." The U.S.—indeed, the world—is increasingly bound by strings of numbers, pictures and words. The storage, retrieval and dissemination of that data is rapidly becoming the stuff of which commerce is made.

Growth in cable television bodes well for job expansion in a number of employment categories. By 1990, the U.S. will require another 17,000 broadcast technicians, the people charged with managing the microphones, video recorders and cameras required for a television or radio broadcast. The burgeoning number of cable channels will create the need for additional television programs. Writers, directors and even actors (believe it or not, Dad) should find more work available.

Spurred by growth in cable television and other communication industries, thousands of jobs may be created in the field of advertising. About 100,000 advertising assistants will be needed by 1990, along with 110,000 advertising and scenario writers in the emerging field of telemarketing. Before we explore telemarketing, be warned that cable television is expected to bring us several variations on the "all commercial" channel. Many companies will begin airing "informercials," product information programs ranging from 30 minutes to several hours. A cheese manufacturer, for example, might present 30 minutes of demonstrations and recipes incorporating its products. Advertising employees face the task of holding the audience's attention for hours, not seconds.

Teletext—which links consumers to data sources via cable or satellite—is another communications field promising growth. Teletext data will include stock quotations, news, banking services, classified advertising and entertainment listings. In a one-way teletext system, a viewer would use a home teletext terminal to scan the news of the day. A two-way arrangement might allow the viewer to deposit and withdraw bank funds, vote and participate in nationwide opinion polls.

It's estimated that by 1990 as much as 20 percent of all

U.S. retail sales will be made via telemarketing, where products are displayed on video screens and orders placed by phone.

Teletext, according to one estimate, will serve 8 million homes by 1990. Strategic, Inc., a San Jose, California, consulting firm, predicts the teletext audience could be as large as 45 million. Omri Serlin, a Strategic vice president, estimates that 45 million teletext customers might require as much as $19 billion in equipment and could pay $16 billion each year for the services.

About 25,000 teletext editors and directors will be needed to edit and direct the presentation of teletext material by 1990. Another 65,000 teletext composition, format and editing specialists will be required to manipulate pictures, graphics and text to deliver the stream of information.

Many people, including some "ink in the veins" newspaper employees, predict teletext may eventually eclipse the traditional gazettes. Although it's doubtful the newspaper will completely disappear, U.S. papers are spending more than $20 million annually on a variety of teletext experiments. With transportation, labor and newsprint costs rising, teletext should make a dent in the newspaper market. Forward-thinking newspaper executives are planning to simply transfer a portion of their news gathering expertise to fill the void. About 167,000 editors, writers and reporters will be needed by 1990 to gather the news—regardless of whether it's printed in newspapers, magazines or on video screens. It's safe to predict that one of the hottest news topics of the future will be (you guessed it) the continuing march of high technology.

Not surprisingly, the computer—just as it will revolutionize offices, factories, hospitals and homes—also will radically alter the movie, art and music industries.

Perhaps the most impressive accomplishments to date have been within the movie industry. Computer-generated imagery (CGI)—the same technique which allows an engineer to design a car on a computer screen—has already made its debut in Hollywood.

In 1982, the magic makers at Walt Disney unveiled *Tron,* a futuristic movie about a maniacal video game, a film brimming with computer-generated scenery, props, and characters. CGI permits moviemakers to create a variety of video wonders, including swift motion, the blending of one object into another and rapidly shifting points of view. Previously, without CGI, even the clever Disney animators were powerless to design such visuals.

By drawing objects on a computer screen, or by programming a number of shapes into the computer and then ordering it to create objects from those shapes, CGI specialists are wowing the movie industry and pushing the art of special effects toward new horizons. The New York Institute of Technology is reportedly at work on a 90-minute film that will be completely computer-generated. Don't be surprised if the Academy of Motion Picture Arts and Sciences eventually awards a computer with an Oscar. Who knows? A silicon chip may be nominated for a Best Supporting role. "Accepting for DXBM 498 is . . ."

We're expected to need about 40,000 computer-assisted graphics layout artists and 40,000 terminal input artists in 1990. Although many of those individuals will work in factories and mills, others will be creating movie magic with CGI.

While computers are finding their niche in the movie industry, some artists are already referring to them as "electronic paintbrushes." Commercial artists are incorporating computers in their work, using light pens to "paint" on video screens. Because computer art systems are still relatively expensive, only a few fine artists are dabbling on electronic easels. But the implications the computer holds for artistic expression—the ability to subtly alter colors or create unworldly shapes—are as plain as the subject's nose in a Grant Wood painting. Therefore, future illustrators and commercial artists can expect the computer to play an important part in their work.

The siren song of electronic expression has not fallen on deaf ears in the music industry, either. Computers, with their ability to translate electric voltages into sound, already provide an eerie musical form. Electronics also is used to alter the sound of conventional instruments. Although some purists argue whether computer painting and music is actually art, others are advancing the computer's contribution a step further—supplying a computer with guidelines and instructing it to compose its own computerized cantata.

The computer-generated imagery we mentioned earlier actually debuted for the mass public long before *Tron* ever hit the movie marquees. Because video games—those quarter-a-time rocket rides into other worlds—owe their roaring monsters and zooming spaceships to CGI. And with CGI's capacity for generating increasingly complex video images, video games are expected to continue enjoying mass popularity.

In fact, many video game authors are now commanding the same celebrity status—and salaries—as best-selling authors. Many video game software writers, who only a few years ago were begging quarters from their parents, are now commanding six-figure incomes for their creations.

Video game sales have topped $1 billion annually and many young program writers are starting their own businesses to get a larger piece of the pie. We'll be needing almost 2 million software writers to meet the nation's demands by 1990. Among that group will be a large contingent of highly creative, handsomely rewarded video game designers. But a few words of caution before you begin writing "The Great American Video Game": Video game players gobble up new games nearly as fast as Pac-Man chews energy dots. Because of the constant demand for new and more challenging games, video game writers may be subject to stress and job burnout. And as the video game market begins to level off, as it did in 1983, competition among video game designers will be fierce.

Speaking of burnout, take lasers . . . please. Lasers are another in a seemingly endless procession of high-tech tools which should have a major impact on the arts and communications industries. "Light scalpels" already are an important device in medicine, where surgeons perform delicate surgery and zap tumors with the concentrated light. Fiber optics, which uses lasers to carry information through glass tubes, is now state-of-the-art in communications.

Perhaps less familiar are the contributions lasers are making in video and sound recording technology. Although the process of recording pictures and sound on a video disc is more than a decade old, the technology only recently reached the point where a computer-controlled laser can record and play back pictures and sound on an erasable, magnetic disc. The disc is reusable and the laser provides the important capability of random access.

Applications for the video disc technology are almost limitless, thus opening a vast area of employment opportunity for any writer or artist with an idea and a potential market. For instance, a mechanic confronted with a sticky service problem might consult a video disc "repair manual." If he tuned in the carburetor section, he'd be treated to a video explanation of the parts and service requirements. The same technology would serve for exercise regimens, dance instruction, furniture refinishing, road maps—virtually any information which lends itself to sound and pictures.

Before we bring down the curtain on communication and art, a final note. Although the competition is fierce and often insurmountable, the few people who reach the pinnacle of the art, entertainment and communications industries stand to become the nation's wealthiest individuals. Movie stars, authors, musicians and athletes already routinely earn millions of dollars annually. Television news personalities, slam-dunking basketball players and good-looking celebrities have all negotiated—and won—multimillion-dollar contracts. As we noted earlier, the odds are long against anyone's hoping to reach the top of such fiercely competitive industries. But for those who make it, the rewards are potentially enormous.

In summary, whether "to be or not to be" an actor, a musician or an artist remains a difficult question in view of

future employment projections. But the following list includes several communications jobs that have received fa-
vorable reviews.

Job Title	Job Numbers	Starting $	Mid $	Education
Teletext Senior Editor and Director	25,000	$30,000	$50,000	4 years college

Much like their counterparts in television, radio and
print, teletext editors and directors will edit the content
and design and direct the presentations offered by teletext
marketing, news and entertainment operations.

| Teletext Computer Assistant Composition, Format and Editing Specialist | 65,000 | $16,000 | $14,000 | 4 years college |

Working under teletext editors and directors, specialists will use computers to manipulate pictures and text in
the presentation of teletext.

| Telemarketing Advertising and Scenario Writer | 110,000 | $18,000 | $35,000 | 4 years college |

A "cousin" of the print and broadcast advertising
copywriters of today will compose advertising text for a
variety of products and services advertised via telemarketing.

| Public Relations Manager | 131,000 | $12,000 | $32,000 | 4 years college |

Although slower than average growth is predicted, more than 130,000 public relations specialists may be needed to write news releases, direct ad campaigns and provide a vital link between companies and organizations on the one hand, and the public and the news media on the other.

| Editor, Writer, and Reporter | 167,000 | $12,000 | $50,000 | 4 years college |

Although the journalism trades are not an area of traditional job growth, the continued proliferation of small daily and weekly newspapers and special-interest magazines and periodicals should provide work for those able to condense stories about the increasingly complex world around them into readable copy.

| Photog- rapher | 91,000 | $14,000 | $21,000 | vocational or 4 years college |

Although slower than average growth is expected in the photography field, technically complicated cameras—including electronic and 3-dimensional cameras—will require the development of a new breed of photographer. While slow growth is expected in the traditional areas of portrait and newspaper photography, better job prospects should be available in areas such as law enforcement and corporate communications.

| Broadcast Technician | 17,000 | $12,000 | $14,000 | vocational |

Involved in the operation and maintenance of equipment used to broadcast radio and television programs. Equipment includes tape recorders, microphones, lights, video cameras and more.

Advertising Assistant	100,000	$10,000	$40,000	4 years college

Works with advertising executives, account representatives, copy writers and others to coordinate and direct advertising campaigns.

Illustrator/Commercial Artist		$10,000	$17,000	vocational or college

Produces illustrations for advertisements used in magazines, newspapers, television, brochures, catalogs, and on books and record album jackets. Also design graphics for television programs and logos for a variety of interests. Computer-generated imagery should play a key role in this job.

Software Writer	1,830,000	$20,000	$30,000	2–4 years college

Software writers will be the catalyst for computer revolutions in a number of industries, including the arts and communication. Without their "orders," or programs, computers are useless. Many of the nearly 2 million writers will be the creators of future video games. The person who hits upon the next "Pac Man" or "Missile Command" stands to make a fortune. Video game sales have already topped $1 billion annually.

Computer-Assisted Graphics (CAG) Terminal Input Artist	40,000	$16,800	$30,000	2 years college/ 2 years voca- tional

While the input artist will work in a variety of print media, using computers to compose type faces and design packaging, the same principles will apply in creating computer-generated imagery for the movies. Although the job will likely have another title, many input artists could find work in the movie, video game and other visual industries.

CAG Graphic Layout Artist	40,000	$10,000	$18,000	2 years college/ 2 years voca- tional

Like the CAG terminal input artist, the layout artist primarily will use a computer to lay out pages of books, magazines, newspapers, record album covers and more. But the same skills could be applied to other tasks, say designing a computer-generated movie set or laying out the battle ground for a new video game.

Parallels can be drawn between the future job prospects for engineers and communicators. Just as the emphasis on math and science skills has suffered in recent years, English, grammar and speech skills have skidded as well.

Declining math and science test scores threaten the technological "brain" of the U.S. Meanwhile, functional illiteracy has become a skull-and-crossbones stamped across the forehead of an increasing number of job seekers. Unable to read directions or complete an employment application, they flounder in the rough seas of a depressed economy.

Although the preceding list promises several hundred thousand jobs for communicators during this decade, only the qualified need apply. Just as the U.S. needs engineers who can comprehend and apply the laws of physics, it needs communicators who speak and write in complete, comprehensible sentences.

In 1981, U.S. Rep. Timothy E. Wirth (D-Colorado) warned of an information age moving forward as an increasingly illiterate populace slides back. "We are in an information society and are going to be more and more dependent upon individuals who can manipulate sophisticated ideas and numbers," Wirth said. "For the first time in history, however, the generation graduating from high school is less literate than its parents."

The electronic revolution has forever changed the way we communicate. As noted in another chapter in this book, computers, printers and a blizzard of related electronic devices are rapidly leading us toward the "paperless office." Electronic machines now give and take bank transactions, issue tickets, print travelers' checks and more. A flock of communication satellites travels the stratosphere, putting exotic locales within reach by telephone and bringing world events home via the television.

Thus, while the arts remain a chancy business for future job seekers, employment growth is projected in several areas of communication.

Cable television is one communications industry riding high on the wave of The Information Age. In 1975, about 9.8 million homes were linked to local cable systems. By 1981, the figure rose to 19.5 million homes. Today, it's estimated that about 77.8 million homes—25 percent of the nation's television homes—are served by more than 4,600 cable companies. It's projected that by 1990 60 percent of the nation's homes will be "hooked on cable." And by 2000, the cable saturation should reach 90 percent or better.

Via a complex network of satellites, antennas and receiving dishes, cable stations feed viewers a smorgasbord of programming ranging from sitcom reruns and first-run movies to religious rallies and sports spectacles. According to one estimate, television satellite capacity should triple by 1984 and demand for broadcasting "space" is expected to quickly surpass the supply.

At the same time, Kathleen Nolan, former president of the Screen Actors Guild, also cautioned against losing our grip on the humanities while we cling to the reins of galloping technology. "At the very time we are exploding with new technologies," she said, "our government is seriously considering major cutbacks in funding for the arts and humanities. Artists must nevertheless lead the way in making the new media not simply computers of mediocre entertainment, but new art forms that express human values in ways appropriate to the particular medium of communication."

What can you and I do to help keep "The Information Age" from being crushed under a tumbling tower of babble? How about paying attention when our high school and college teachers diagram sentences and conjugate verbs? And what about resisting the tendency to "-ize," "-wise" and otherwise bastardize the language?

English, grammar, and writing and speaking courses should be mandatory requirements right through college and vocational school. With the advent of computer-based education, students could easily become proficient in these areas at their own pace. As parents, we should insist that communication skills be mainstream requirements and make sure kids read books as fun rather than work. As business people, we can use simple, direct sentences.

Best of all, we can all take the time to be competent communicators and then spread the good words.

6

FACTORIES AND MANUFACTURING

The Changing American Scene

Cincinnati, Youngstown, Columbus, Rockford, Peoria, Decatur, Detroit, Flint, Dearborn.

This roster of Midwest cities reads like a lineup of once vigorous, heavy-hitting auto industry "all-stars" now humbled by a strong, young pitcher in a new economic "game."

New rules—cheap labor, import-export quotas, government concessions—have baffled U.S. manufacturers while foreign competitors scored impressive gains. U.S. factories have been slow to pick up on an important industrial "change-up:" automation, robotics, factory upgrading, shared management. And the American "players"—both business and labor—contributed to their own demise by becoming "fat," demanding too much money for sometimes inferior work.

Employment statistics reveal the "game's" outcome. General Motors closed more than 200 plants and laid off almost 150,000 workers in 1981–1983. When Ford closed its San Jose, California, assembly plant in summer 1983, a single shift of 2,250 workers at GM's Van Nuys plant remained the only working automakers in a state that once claimed 20,000.

By no means has the auto industry been the only "strike-out" victim among the nation's manufacturing industries. No fewer than 5,000 factories have locked their gates since 1975.

North Carolina lost 17 percent of its textile jobs during the past 10 years. Many of those shifted to Cambodia, Singapore and Thailand, where 15-cents-an-hour labor is available. Automation replaced many other jobs. North Carolina's Richmond County hosts the world's most modern textile plant, a $45-million "factory of the future" where looms spin polyester fabric using a jet of water instead of a hand-operated shuttle. The machines produce fabric 3 times faster than 10 years ago. Where once a textile worker had responsibility for 2 looms, each worker now oversees the work of 55 robot looms.

It's predicted that American factory employment will decline for the remainder of this decade. Not long ago, 1 of every 3 Americans worked in factories. By 1990, no more than 1 of every 5 U.S. jobs will be filled by factory workers, if the prognosticators are right.

Tragically, human lives are buried under the numbers. A Toledo couple, unable to find work in Ohio, committed suicide in Texas in 1982 after they ran out of cash and hope in their search for work.

So what lies ahead? Continued doom and despair? The answer is: yes and no. Unless American factory workers accept lower wages, factories become more productive, managers become more creative and "Made in the U.S.A." becomes an attractive label to foreign buyers, additional bad news is likely. No end to the loss of factory jobs is forecast before 1990.

At the same time, American factories are poised for an

unprecedented surge in productivity via new, sophisticated automation. From 1971 to 1980, productivity in U.S. factories rose by 85 percent. During the next 5 years, productivity should spurt by 200 percent as robots and other automative tools take their places on the lines.

Initially, robots may deliver a devastating blow to the factory work force. Robot planners estimate a robot can replace the equivalent of about 2.5 people per shift, about 4.5 people on 2 shifts and 6 people on 3 shifts. Yet as robot prices decline and industry turns increasingly to these "mechanical men," a brave new work force should be generated to design, produce, control and service robots. According to one estimate, it takes 2 to 4 years of "people work"—somewhere in the national economy—to install a robot in a U.S. factory. Servicing and adjusting that robot provides more work for factory personnel.

The push-pull of the figures is apparent. For example, the Upjohn Institute for Employment Research estimates that robots will eliminate as many as 24,000 auto jobs in Michigan alone by 1990. Upjohn, however, also predicts that as many as 18,000 new jobs will be created as Michigan's new robotics industry—which helped create the employment void—now expands to help fill the job gap. The institute also projects Michigan's auto industry will need about 3,500 robot engineers by 1990.

It looks like U.S. industry is beginning to grasp both the benefits and side-effects of the automation trend. American automakers, for instance, are installing robots at a fast clip and are exhibiting renewed vigor partly because of automation. General Motors, meanwhile, has pledged $120 million annually for retraining workers who lose their jobs to robots. The employees can leave their jobs on the assembly line and, with proper training, step into positions as robot mechanics, technicians, producers and controllers.

The robotics revolution will affect not only the auto industry, but also many other manufacturers. General Electric, Westinghouse, International Business Machines, United Technologies and Bendix all have announced plans to produce robots which they envision running the factories of the future while creating more jobs than they destroy. Especially in the area of robotics, many jobs will be made for salespersons, marketers and exporters of robots.

Robots eventually will dispose of radioactive and toxic waste, explore and mine outer space, harvest crops, handle hazardous manufacturing materials like asbestos and help test new viruses in medical research labs.

With the advent of robotics, there are likely to be what the automobile industry calls "permanent replacements" among the factory work force. But with attrition and attention to retraining, it's hoped that robotics will prove an evolution, rather than an end point, for U.S. factory employment. The U.S. Department of Labor is writing regulations to allocate $25 million to state governments for retraining displaced workers. Funds for the program come under the Job Training Partnership Act, effective October 1, 1983, which is expected to emphasize training over "make-work" expenditures which characterized many past jobs programs.

Robots won't be the only new machines in U.S. factories during the coming years. Lasers, for example, are expected to do many of the cutting and shaping tasks once performed by cumbersome drills, punches and other metal-working machinery. About 600,000 laser technicians will be needed by 1990 to handle these new machines.

Fiber optics will become essential to the inspection and quality-control equipment in factories of the future. Some aircraft manufacturers already use fiber optic testing equipment to check airplane parts alignment. More than 40,000 fiber optics technicians must be trained to handle the equipment by the end of this decade.

Production of alternative energy fuels is a virtually untapped source of employment opportunity. How many people might we employ if coal slurry, shale oil, tar sands, peat, synthetic and solar fuels become marketable forms of energy?

On the other hand, little or no growth is expected in a number of current job categories, including sheet metal worker, pattern maker, punch press and stamping operator and textile machine operator. It's projected that the U.S.

will need about 1.67 million assemblers by 1990, although that figure represents slower than average growth for the job category.

The coming changes in U.S. manufacturing are symbolized in the comparison of employment prospects for 2 job categories: welders/cutters and laser technicians. Although the nation is expected to need about 692,000 additional welders and cutters by 1990, that figure represents only a slower than average growth rate. At the same time, in a new job classification, about 600,000 laser technicians must be trained in order to satisfy industry demands during this decade. Starting welders can expect to earn about $22,000. Beginning laser technicians will likely earn about $30,000 per year.

The following list includes a number of job categories, like laser technician, which will be found in the "line-ups" of the future as U.S. manufacturers and factories learn the rules and become competitive in a new industrial game.

Job Title	Job Numbers	Starting $	Mid $	Education
Laser Technician	600,000	$15,000	$25,000	2 years vocational

Operates, troubleshoots and repairs industrial lasers that cut and weld metal parts, drill holes in metal frames and align machinery along fast-moving assembly lines. Will replace many of today's tool and foundry workers, especially in plants where robots are assembled.

Electronics Technician	200,000	$14,000	$22,000	2 years vocational

Applies electronic theory, principles of transistorized circuitry and electrical testing procedures to lay out, build, test, troubleshoot and modify the endless number of new electronic products.

Electronics Assembler	100,000	$12,000	$18,000	high school

Uses hand tools, soldering irons, etc., to assemble radios, television sets, video recorders, video games and other electronic products.

Holographic Inspector	200,000	$20,000	$28,000	2 years college

The non-destructive testing job of the future. Automated factories that use optical fibers to sense light, temperature, pressure, viscosity and dimension will transmit measurements to computers to compare data with stored holographic (3-dimensional) models. Comparisons will be read by inspectors trained in the art and science of holography.

Fiber Optics Technician	40,000	$11,000	$19,000	2 years vocational

A job already initiated in aircraft plants to check alignments of ailerons, landing gear and other plane components. Nuclear power plants also may use fiber optics to monitor temperatures, pressures and control rod levels. The world's telephone companies are sure to be a big employer of technicians as fiber optics replace copper cables.

Energy Technician	650,000	$13,000	$26,000	2 years college

Jobs in energy-generating plants will increase dramatically as alternative fuels, including nuclear power, coal slurry, shale oil, tar sands and synthetic fuels, become marketable. Retraining will be essential. Toledo Edison trains its nuclear plant personnel with computers so training can be updated quickly as jobs change.

Energy Auditor	180,000	$11,500	$15,600	2 years voca-tional

Will use infrared cameras to detect warm and cold spots in factories and work to control heating and cooling costs. Will work with engineers to manage energy conservation and control systems for office buildings, large apartment complexes and factories.

Computer-Assisted Manufac-turing (CAM) Specialist	300,000	$20,000	$31,000	2 years college

Uses computer skills to monitor machinery running on a computerized program of instructions. Will make sure the instructions are complete and precise. Will watch over a battery of controls and printouts to ensure manufacturing procedures are correct.

CAM Mechanic	300,000	$12,500	$19,500	2 years voca-tional

Will install and test machine tools wired into computers to make sure they follow computerized factory functions through every step of the manufacturing process. Must be a sure-fingered mechanic with rudimentary understanding of computers. Will be one of the most common jobs in the "Factory of the Future."

CAM Tool Technician	170,000	$14,000	$19,000	2 years voca-tional

Installs special tools, jigs, fixtures, spray nozzles and machine parts to be used in inert atmospheres, in acid and alkaline atmospheres. Equivalent of the old tool-and-die maker working in computer-aided manufacturing.

CAM Production Scheduler	90,000	$12,300	$18,400	2 years voca- tional

Monitors rate of production schedule on CAM line so assembly line doesn't stop, back up or speed up to the point where production functions are missed or go incomplete.

CAM Production Superin- tendent	90,000	$15,000	$25,000	2 years voca- tional

Equivalent of the old shop foreman. Supervises mechanics, schedulers, tool installers, inventory clerks and parts planners at individual computer-aided work stations throughout the factory.

Software Coordi- nator	80,000	$17,000	$25,000	2 years college

Integrates computer programmed instructions for machines and installs them in wiring that connects computers and machine tools. The factory link with software writers. Makes changes in computerized assembly line, also.

CAM Traffic Controller	20,000	$11,500	$14,500	2 years college

Integrates factory parts made by outside subcontractors with parts finished internally. Formerly called materials control clerk.

| CAM Inventory Supervisor | 14,500 | $11,500 | $14,500 | 2 years voca- tional |

Computerizes factory inventory, much the way stock clerks do now. Will need to learn a new "language" and may use more computer lexicon in everyday conversation than anybody else in the factory.

| Materials Utilization Technician | 400,000 | $15,000 | $24,000 | 2 years college |

Will handle, process, machine and fabricate many new synthetic materials created to replace scarce, high-priced metals and other materials unsuited for new manufacturing technology. The precursors of this job are the people employed by Lockheed Aircraft Corporation and Rockwell to manufacture and install silicon glass tiles to cover the fuselage of the space shuttle and protect the craft from the searing heat of re-entry.

| Robot Production Technician | 800,000 | $15,000 | $24,000 | 2 years college |

Tends the robots performing an endless variety of tasks on the assembly lines of the future. Skills will include understanding how robots are constructed, how their hands and arms move and how computer programs that control robot movements are composed.

| Robot Program- mers | 200,000 | $11,500 | $19,500 | 2 years college |

Will reprogram computers with new instructions as robots move to different sections or are called on to perform new tasks.

| Robot Checkout Technician | 250,000 | $12,500 | $22,500 | 2 years voca- tional |

Will put the robot through a prescribed sequence of hand and arm movements to make sure the robot is performing its task properly. Will require a long training program with emphasis on safety. In the only known serious accident involving a robot and its "keeper," a Japanese technician was decapitated by the swift and accidental movement of a robot's arm.

| Robot Repairman | 140,000 | $14,000 | $22,500 | 2 years voca- tional |

A combination electrician/plumber who can troubleshoot a malfunctioning robot to ensure its electrical wiring is working, its pneumatic feed lines are secure and its hydraulic arms and hands are working properly.

| Robot Engineer | 450,000 | $14,700 | $35,000 | 4 years college |

Designs and installs a robot to perform a particular job. One of the most challenging jobs of the future, with nearly unlimited opportunities for an engineer with creativity and imagination.

| Sales Represen- tative Manu- facturing | 440,000 | $16,000 | $37,000 | 4 years college |

Visits prospective buyers to provide information about a product, demonstrate it, and (if all goes well) finally sell it. Nearly all manufacturers employ sales representatives.

| Industrial Hygiene Technician | 70,000 | $12,500 | $16,400 | 4 years college |

Responsible for safety programs and general sanitation at a manufacturing concern. Job is especially important at plants handling hazardous or volatile material.

Before we close this examination of future manufacturing job prospects, a few more comments may serve to illustrate even more clearly the impact robots are expected to have on U.S. factories.

Japan first began putting robots on its assembly lines in the early 1970s. Now, with 14,000 working robots, Japan boasts 60 percent of the world's production robots.

The Japanese noticed early on that robots not only perform many tasks more efficiently than humans, but also do it without the health risks humans can face.

In Japan's automobile factories, robots have been using only 60 percent of the paint once used by humans to paint a new auto. The 40 percent savings is only one reason Japan's automakers are able to out-sell their Detroit competitors.

In assembling cars, robots are more precise than people. Instead of working at human tolerances of one-eighth or one-sixteenth of an inch, robots work at tolerances of one-thousandth of an inch. The Japanese also found that robots waste only 1 percent of the metal they cut. Humans lose as much as 15 percent to scrap.

Taking its cue from the Japanese, GM plans to use robots not only for painting and welding, but also for assembly and subassembly of car bodies, engines, alternators, chassis and brakes.

One GM study estimates the company may save as much as $25 million annually by using robots instead of humans to install windshields, because robots drop fewer windshields and don't miss work because of injuries from mishandled glass.

Of course, in many ways, robots are like computers.

Without us people, where would they be? The increase in productivity through robotics will not be had without much research and development, testing, education, training, planning and designing. That's where humans come in.

Skills will be needed both to manufacture robots and to keep them working. There is little room in the robotics business—or almost any other future business—for high school dropouts. Training will be a must, education an essential. Because even though U.S. factories will eventually field a strong "team" of robots, humans will remain the "clean-up hitters" in manufacturing.

7

RETRAINING
FOR THE
NEW WORLD
OF WORK

Twenty years ago, the talk was of retooling American industrial plants. Today, the talk is of retooling American workers, American schools and American training systems.

This represents one of the most significant attitude changes to evolve in the 20th century, and its impending impact on us creates rumor, fear, speculation and excitement.

It also leads to some new rules. People will have to "learn how to learn," to think and to communicate more effectively than ever before, and they will have to be able to do so with a flexibility to match the fast-changing demands made on them by the workplace of the future. People will have to learn how to relearn a skill and how to adapt it in a constantly changing and evolving job, and they will have to do it the rest of their employment lives. Workers will no longer be stifled in rigidly defined jobs where only one function is ever demanded of them; jobs will stay interesting as workers learn, relearn and adapt their skills.

Today, even our educational systems and institutions grapple with structural change.

From kindergarten through graduate school, public and private schools, colleges and universities face unbelievable and sometimes unbearable problems and challenges: shifting and aging student populations, too few babies to support the explosion of academic growth caused by the earlier baby booms, teachers and professors fleeing to business and industry where the pay is more and the grief is less, lack of government funds and supportive taxpayers.

And, then, adding insult to injury, these same schools, colleges and vocational facilities constantly must defend against the charge that they are "educating" people right into illiteracy.

It's enough to make you wonder why anyone would want to sit on a school board, much less lecture in a classroom.

Still, the age-old premise that the fate of empires rests on the education of youth is somehow even more appropriate today.

How workers prepare for jobs and careers demands a revolution. Otherwise, it's back to hunting and fishing and there's not much future in that. No, retooling American workers is the only way to go and that push is on for a variety of reasons.

The first reason, of course, is that necessity is the mother of invention. With unemployment hovering at 10 percent in the early 1980s and as high as 20 percent or more in one-industry cities like Flint, Michigan (autos), and Hibbing, Minnesota (mining), and unemployment benefits running out, old skills must be converted to new ones so the job search can begin.

Simply put, many of the old jobs have disappeared and

not because robots and computers infiltrated and upstaged them. Manufacturing will consume only 11 percent of the jobs in the year 2000, a real crash from 28 percent in 1980; agriculture-related occupations will shrink by 25 percent to 3 percent from 4 percent. Put into disturbingly clear numbers, more than 1.2 million of the more than 11 million unemployed in the recent recession will never again set foot in their old plants in the automobile, steel, textile, rubber or railroad industries.

Because business failed to improve plant productivity, because workers insisted upon the growth of paychecks rather than the accumulation of skills and because international competition closed in, factory jobs moved to Japan, Korea, Hong Kong and India. This is called structural unemployment and the only real way to combat it is to get prepared for the new structure.

From now on a strong basic education, higher education, training and retraining will become an accepted part of our work routine, especially as the Information Age with its high tech tools takes hold.

But what kind of education really leads to the much-coveted career?

And how should we prepare for and insist upon retraining? Especially in a society that has long loved education and long spurned vocational training? The answer: it depends.

If you take a good hard look at where the jobs are going to be, you can assume attitudes about vocational training will alter. Nearly every new job classification predicted ends in the word technician. Robotics, health, engineering technicians. Remember, Japan has one-twentieth the lawyers, one-seventh the accountants, but 5 times as many engineers as the U.S. The Bureau of Labor Statistics predicts that within the next 10 years, 80 percent of the available jobs will require some kind of after-high school education and, of them, 80 percent will require something other than or in addition to a traditional liberal arts education.

Vocational and technical training soon will rank up there with the other basic skills of reading, writing, math and science. Already, the computer literacy movement, a forerunner of modern technical training, carries with it the fervor of a populist political campaign. Pre-schoolers, elementary and high school students comfortably use computer terminals to study and problem-solve. Five Minnesota colleges, Hamline University, St. Thomas College, Augsburg College, St. John's University and St. Catherine's College, banded together recently into a "computer literacy consortium" to help their students plunge into the world of technical and electronic employment. A well-known national marketing firm surveyed 15,000 high schools in early 1983 and found that a majority of them were expanding their vocational/technical studies at a greater rate than any other discipline.

Those of us who are a little older, who have already been trained and are working, often hang onto an archaic notion of what vocational/technical training really is. Our memories call up images of welding, automobile repairing, overhauling motors, installing air conditioning and refrigeration, plumbing and heating—"shop" we used to call it. In those days, people thought the only kids who went on to vocational schools were the hoods, the greasers, the dropouts and the college rejects.

Those were the days of *American Graffiti* and they're gone. The image of vocational/technical training has improved because the jobs of the future are improving, despite how gloomy the doomsayers sound right now.

The ways in which we will learn and train are as futuristic as the jobs we'll be learning and training for, and they will often involve the use of a computer.

Computer-based education and training was introduced as early as 1970, but only recently started to win converts.

Again, it was almost a matter of necessity. Old teaching methods centered around books and classroom instructors take too much time to combat the rising unemployment figures, to accommodate the modernization of work.

But, electronic publishing, which uses computers to prepare and distribute materials, requires much less time than traditional book publishing to disseminate knowledge. The traditional approach of collecting information, finding an author, writing, printing and marketing can burn up 3 to 5 years. By the time a book hits the library shelf or classroom, it is outdated. In the Information Age, more than ever, time is progress. Only by using the computer to publish and distribute knowledge can we really hope to quickly retrain and re-educate people and keep them current and working.

Many schools, colleges and universities now use computer-based education to aid teachers in the classroom, especially in some of the basic skills areas. Kids seem to like computer-based education because it makes them a class of one: Students sit at their own terminals to study lessons, take tests and review in privacy and at their own pace. Advanced students can move more quickly and not get bored, while average students can move more slowly and not be embarrassed. The teacher, meanwhile, gains time to work with students individually and prepare more interesting learning plans.

Business and industry is gravitating toward new retraining methods as well, most of them offering skills development for the first time. From now on, those of us already in the job market and the new workers joining us should plan to learn new skills and polish up old ones each year. We predict workers will "turnover" careers every decade with major revisions occurring every 2 years.

To the surprise of many, the automobile industry is leading the way. General Motors, for example, uses PLATO computer-based education to train workers in current factory processes and to teach them new skills such as robotics. Because employees can interweave training with working, thanks to the computers on-site, both the company and the workers benefit. The company saves training and production losses associated with traditional classroom instruction, and the workers learn skills for the future while collecting a paycheck in the here and now.

General Motors currently spends about $125 million on retraining, and the demand is so great the company recently purchased its own computer system and 200 terminals to bring skills training to even more employees.

Slowly, companies are beginning to see that by saving workers from the scrap heap they can actually be an asset if retrained cost-effectively to handle the tools of the new technology such as CAD/CAM.

Other progressive companies/institutions—American Airlines, United Airlines, Merck, Sharpe and Dohme, General Mills, Dupont, Westinghouse, AT&T, the U.S. Coast Guard and the U.S. Army—lead the way in pioneering new training methods.

One company, Winnebago Industries in Forest City, Iowa, formed a partnership with Control Data Corp. to bring computer-based education to the city's schools and to the Winnebago plants.

Like the school kids, workers also gravitate toward computer-based training once the usual computer anxiety eases. Again, by training individually on the terminal, each person goes as fast or as slow as he or she needs to. This privacy factor, coupled with the feeling of being in charge of your own training, usually results in more effective training. For many of us who are years removed from the classroom, the very thought of appearing stupid or slow is too painful.

In some cases, it may seem that computers are also responsible for people losing their jobs, and in some cases it's true. Robots that cost $3 an hour to run and maintain certainly produce a less expensive product than people who cost $20 an hour. But those robots need to be programmed, maintained, installed and "managed" on the line, and new jobs are created. First of all, those robots have to be built—again, new jobs. Computers didn't eliminate bank tellers and airline reservationists, but they raised the number of services offered and made it necessary for those employees to upgrade their skills to keep their jobs. If properly managed, this shift to the Information/Service Age can increase the number of jobs as well as their quality. If not, however, better jobs will be lost, and low service jobs will be left.

If you think you're too old to learn new skills or how to study again, it's time to put those thoughts behind you. As business, government and schools begin to work cooperatively rather than competitively, retraining will become a welcome way of life.

In the future, nearly 4 percent of all workers will be in some kind of training program each year. In addition, the shrinking number of available workers, because of a rapidly declining birth rate, means we will be needed longer to keep America pumping products and services. At the same time, the increase in productivity resulting from falling production prices and higher output because of new technology will give us more free time over that longer span to put some balance into our lives.

Yes, right now, and looking into the 21st century, technical professions seem to be the best bet. Each year, the United States graduates only one-fifth the number of engineers taking their place at the drawing boards in Japan. Another 50,000 or so leave for other fields because they seek change or change has done them in.

The telecommunications, computer and health care industries alone will absorb millions of technocrats by 2000. Without them, those industries will fail. Jobs will disappear.

Ford Motor Company still hires nearly 1,000 college and university graduates a year, and most of them are engineers or MBAs.

Does this apparently unending appetite for science and other precision backgrounds mean we should rush solely for vocational training?

No, absolutely not. As important as math, science and vocational skills are, they alone are not enough. What was true when we were children, as it was when our parents were children, is still fact. Not everything changes.

Because in order for you and me to be equipped to change, we also still need the "thinking-cap" skills. We must insist upon learning about decision-making, problem-solving, creativity, communications, critical thinking, evaluation, analysis, how to consider several ideas and merge them into an outstanding one. These skills turn "jobs" into "careers."

And if you can't write down your ideas in short, simple sentences without inventing new words, you will be lost in the information society and it will be lost on you. Already, our "well-educated" chief executives, who were taught better, depend on industry lingo to get their ideas across the board room table and into your homes. It may be laziness or snobbery, but the lapse causes a gap between buyer and seller that hurts our economic growth and prosperity.

Across the land, teachers, parents, students, business leaders debate these issues: Is Socrates still compatible with 64K microchip technology? Does it matter if Johnny and Joanie understand the theory of addition if the computer gives them the right answer? Does classical music soothe the savage beast *and* contribute to job security and productivity? Should teachers be paid more *and* given seniority/security rights? How do we encourage the above-average students as well as the average students?

Whatever else happens, one thing is sure: Students will be expected to perform better and longer than they did in the past and so will their instructors.

The President's Report on Excellence in Education in April 1983 hinted of things to come. Among other things, the report recommended for high school students: (a) 7 hours of class a day rather than the current 5; (b) 220 days of school rather than the current 180; (c) 4 years of English; (d) 3 years of math and science; (e) 2 years of a foreign language; and (f) two years of computer science. Apparently, someone is hearing the message that Russian school children require 7 years of these subjects compared to our paltry 2 1/2 years in high school.

We're learning pretty quickly that wars can be won in the classroom as well as on the battlefield.

We'd like to tell you that you'll always be in the job you and your children have now or are studying for. Frankly, we can't. We'd like to tell you that the automobile plants, steel plants, garment plants will rebound to their previously high levels. But that would be a dreamer's wish.

What we can tell you is how to learn about education, training and retraining and how to go about getting the right combination: Ask tough questions.

FOR VOCATIONAL TRAINING

1. As you plan your future, be sure to work in a mix of academic and vocational training.

2. What is the quality of training? How relevant are the courses? Are they regularly reviewed and updated so that the training is current, well-rounded and of a high quality? Who are the instructors? Do they have actual work experience in the career field they teach? What about the school? How long has it been established? What is the size of the average class?

3. Will you really learn the practical skills you'll need on the job? How much of the training is theoretical; how much of it is practical "hands-on" experience working with real computers and other equipment you're likely to encounter in a future job?

4. How responsive is the program to the individual? Will you be locked into a class? Or will you be allowed to progress, within the framework of a schedule, at your own learning pace? Will an instructor be available to work with you, one-to-one, when you need help? Will you be competing against the norm or against the goals and timetable you set for yourself? Can you attend evening and weekend classes?

5. What is the cost of tuition? Are there extra charges for books, fees or equipment? What is the cost per hour of training? What are the terms of payment? What is the school's refund policy? Do you pay only for the hours taken?

6. Is the school accredited? Has it been examined by trade and/or education associations which set

training standards? Does it meet their demanding educational, professional and business criteria? Is the school licensed by the state?

7. Does the school assist you in obtaining financial aid? What types of financial aid programs are offered? Are government financial programs available?

8. What is the graduation and placement rate? How many students actually complete the program? What percentage of students get jobs in the field for which they were trained? Does the school provide current placement information in writing? If so, are the statistics measured on a consistent basis? How recent are the statistics?

9. What kind of placement assistance, if any, does the school offer? How does it provide this assistance? How is the school set up to help its graduates seek jobs? Are job development skills, including interviewing techniques and resume writing, part of the curriculum? What types of jobs do graduates obtain? What is the range of starting salaries?

10. Does the school have strict admission standards? What are its academic requirements? Does it test students prior to admission to determine their potential for a particular course of study?

11. Does the school provide refresher courses?

IN HIGH SCHOOLS

1. Does the school balance requirements between math, science and the languages?

2. What average SAT and ACT scores are the school's students achieving?

3. Does the school rate academic achievements as highly as athletic prowess?

4. What percentage of the school population goes on to college or intensive vocational training?

5. Does the school attempt to teach kids about jobs in the future and the importance of technical skills?
6. Does the school use computers and other modern equipment?
7. Does the student counseling staff match advice to ability and tomorrow's job market? Does it encourage girls and boys equally?
8. Does the school hold "career days" or make certain students get some exposure to business and "real-world" experience?
9. Is the school offering computer literacy?
10. How much of your tax dollar goes to the school system?
11. Is there an active PTA?

FOR COLLEGES OR UNIVERSITIES

1. Does the major you choose demand a balance in technical, writing, communications and evaluation skills?
2. Are there placement services available and what kind of results have they produced?
3. Do you know any graduates who could tell you how their education has held up under the pressures of the changing job market and economic climate?
4. Does the faculty include a mix of academic and practicing professionals?
5. Are internship programs available? Does the school work hard to get its students into internships?
6. Does the institution highly regard such measuring sticks as a dean's list and advanced programs for gifted students?
7. How large is the library? What access does it have to data bases?

8. If you had to transfer, would your credits be easily accepted by another school?
9. Are computers used? Do private businesses support the school with services and equipment?
10. Has the program taught you to think, to challenge, to question, to probe?
11. Have you learned to assess your own weaknesses and strengths?
12. What is the school's ability to provide scholarships and financial aid?
13. Does it work closely with the business community?

After all the analyzing, contemplating and searching, you may think getting education and vocational training is harder and riskier than getting a job.

But stick in there, it's going to get better. While the debate rages on about the best education to get the best job and to become the best citizen, remember this: Plato tried to stop students from listening to Homer.

Despite the problems, confusion and competition, the world of learning can be and possibly will be your world forever. And it's going to be more fun and give us a break from the rigors of constant working.

As our society realizes trained workers are an investment in our marketplace, not an expense, teachers will be better rewarded financially and socially. That will lure back some of the best teachers who walked out of classrooms in search of a decent living and a little respect.

Schools and business and industry will form partnerships to produce better education workers. Even today, companies like Hallmark, Honeywell, IBM, Winnebago Industries, Apple Computer, Control Data Corp. are lending and giving materials and grants to schools in exchange for research, testing sites and skilled future workers. Company laboratories, now secretive and mysterious, will share materials, experiments and knowledge with the best and brightest students.

Instead of duplicating services, some colleges, universities, vocational schools, even high schools, will share facilities and specializations. Professional practitioners will teach alongside academic professionals, giving students a chance to debate, probe and challenge as they never have before.

Increasingly, schools, colleges and universities will pay tribute to "chemletes" and "mathletes" as well as athletes. Students should receive letters in math, physics, chemistry, communications and vocationally related extracurricular activities, similar to athletic letters. Finally, dollars will be poured into computers, not just stadiums.

Government, sooner or later, will convert to brain power from military power. The 1983 presidential look at the country's educational structure will mushroom into government support in the form of tax credits and the sale of the government's massive data base.

Those of us who were lucky enough to land jobs will slip in and out of school more easily than any generation before us. Never again will people over 30 lament about losing their studying skills. Soon, workers' bonuses will be based partially on the willingness to relearn. The chance to go to school will be like vacation—it will renew our energy, restore our creativity, increase our productivity.

For a list of colleges and universities be sure to check the appendices at the end of this book. Also included are the names and addresses of state departments or associations that can provide you with information about technical and vocational schools. It's hard to believe that in this time of concern about education and training no national data base of schools exists. But there are many ways to get at the information if you have determination.

Ongoing education and training means better informed voters, more productive workers, more skilled decision-makers and communicators. And you will fit right into this idyllic scene if you just remember the basics:

- Learn to read and write effectively.
- Learn to communicate simply.

- Learn to manage information instead of it managing you.
- Learn computer literacy as well as functional literacy.
- Learn your history and relate it to your future.
- Learn a job skill.
- Learn to learn.
- Learn to think.
- And learn how to do it for the rest of your life.

8

HOW TO GET AND KEEP A JOB

Department of Labor statistics clearly spotlight a dilemma: in October 1981, 110,000 jobs went unfilled even though unemployment figures rose. Nearly all the openings were for blue-collar and clerical employees, those tracked most faithfully by the Labor Department. So if you were also to capture the number of white-collar positions open for the taking, the proof would be even more dramatic.

Of the reported openings, 67,000 were in the sales and clerical areas, and 49,000 were in the service sector. Heading the list of in-demand jobs were auto mechanics, clerk typists, restaurant cooks, materials handlers, secretaries and waitresses. These openings weren't bound by geography; generally they were spread across the entire country.

Even today, many job postings calling for skilled labor go unheeded simply because there is a growing shortage of trained, skilled workers in our factories, offices, hospitals and research labs.

And, good news, the demand for workers is going to grow even more. By the early 1990s, shortages are predicted in a number of key industries. Labor Department papers report that while the U.S. will need far fewer shoe repairmen, gas station operators and postal clerks by 1990, it will be searching for increased numbers of computer technicians, systems analysts, home health aides.

What the world really needs is a modern-day Fanny Brice, who goes about pushing people into jobs rather than into marriages. Short of that miracle worker, however, getting and keeping a job is a process that can be learned and performed individually throughout a lifetime. Headhunting firms can help, but you've got to know how to manage them, too.

Many technical institutes, like Control Data Institutes and DeVry Technical Institutes, insist that their students take and pass aggressive personal marketing programs that teach skills in landing a job.

The first step, of course, is obvious: become well-trained and educated for a career. As soon as possible, whether that be in high school or when a career has stalled or a job ended, the search to isolate areas of interest and ability should begin. For some people, this is as easy and natural as breathing; for others, the search for vocational interests and aptitudes ends in frustration, anger and confusion.

Constructing a career isn't unlike constructing a building in many ways. Tools of the trade exist for both and, if used properly, can build a firm foundation. Guidance counselors in high schools, colleges and vocational schools often hoard away valuable research materials such as job trend analyses, employment forecasts, guidelines for isolating interests, sending "pitch" letters, and well-written resumes with a marketing bent, and how-to-succeed tips for interviewing. These educational advisers, along with private employment counselors, public agencies funded by state and local governments, and nonprofit agencies, can provide and administer basic interest and aptitude tests to help job-seekers and planners find themselves. Many times, these tools cost little or nothing.

Once you've found your heart's desire when it comes to jobs, you can look for the right training and educational facility to earn job-preparation skills.

Sometimes, though, getting ready for a job seems a snap when compared to signing on for a job. Record-high, unbelievably high, unemployment the last few years combined with shifting employment markets to turn job search into a figurative elusive butterfly. People who took finding a job for granted in the 1950s, 1960s and 1970s never developed good job-seeking skills, never suspected the "selling" of themselves would be similar to selling a product or service. The Great Depression, with its massive unemployment and food lines, retreated into a national memory that hoped it was a fluke. While the United States swallowed up its own resources to feed the greatest economic boom this world had ever seen, the issues of jobs and joblessness surfaced only during occasional, though ever more frequent, bouts of recession.

Now, those issues are page one in major newspapers throughout the country, cover stories in national magazines and perturbing visual images on the evening television news. It's no wonder today's younger generations, those in high schools as well as in colleges, worry more about a good job, a good living and a good bank account than about war, peace, civil rights and other "nonmaterial" concerns.

Finding a job today requires diligence, stubbornness, discipline and salesmanship. Keeping one demands ongoing training, awareness of changing job trends and flexibility. On the next few pages, you'll find some tips for getting and keeping a job. Included in the appendices are samples of a strong, standard resume, pitch letter and thank-you letter that can be used in your job hunt.

1. Make a list of perspective employers, including all those who employ people with your skills. Include

all potential employers on this list even if they are not currently recruiting. Be sure to check the newspaper want ads, local or regional business and employment shoppers, the business Yellow Pages, and bulletin boards on college campuses, in vocational schools and in state Manpower and employment agencies.

2. Prepare a straightforward, neatly typed and short resume. Whole books have been devoted to resume-writing (one of the best is *What Color is Your Parachute!*), but the basics are the same.

- Be accurate.
- Put education section before experience section if it is your strongest selling point, and vice versa.
- Include phonetic spelling of your name if it is difficult to pronounce.
- List a telephone number where you can be reached and when.
- Write positively about yourself (using words like active, adaptable, energetic, enthusiastic, loyal, systematic, forceful, disciplined, creative, tactful, talented, reliable, self-reliant, etc.).
- Keep the resume short—one or two pages—and do the same with sentences and paragraphs.
- Include your entire career since high school.
- Be creative.
- Exclude information which would limit your scope: salary or geographic preferences, availability dates, names of references.

3. Place personal calls to the companies you are interested in, asking for a personnel person or, even better, the head of the department or area in which you wish to work. Keep the conversation brief and go for the sale—an interview. Promise to send a resume.

4. Prepare a cover letter for your resume, including the following:

- Your previous telephone conversation, if you had one.

- Your job objective.
- A brief overview statement of your qualifications or primary attributes as they relate specifically to the job in question.
- Your willingness to be flexible.
- Your plan to follow up with a telephone call, stating clearly the date you will call to set up the interview.

5. Learn and rehearse interviewing techniques.
   - Listen carefully to the interviewer's questions and answer them as succinctly and briefly as possible. If you don't understand a question, ask for clarification.
   - Learn how to get your messages across while answering questions. A good approach is to memorize the five key things you would like the interviewer to hear about you and work them subtlely into the discussion.
   - Again, use positive, active words.
   - Share comments from others about your work.
   - Mention any work awards or recognition you received.
   - Don't distract the interviewer by smoking, chewing gum, fiddling in a briefcase, purse or file, gazing out a window, winding your watch, etc.
   - At the close of the interview, ask for further direction.
   - Dress conservatively, but well, with unwrinkled suits, shirts, dresses, polished shoes, neat ties.

6. Send a thank-you letter after the interview.
   - Thank the interviewer for the time and chance to present yourself.
   - Reinforce your interest in the position and the basic skills which qualify you for it.
   - Compliment the organization.
   - State when you will call if you have not heard from the interviewer.

7. Follow through with everything you say you will do.

8. Stick to your plan and be sure to keep working with the employers you are most interested in. Setting up a separate timetable chart can help you meet deadlines and track your progress.

Once you've found and started a job, you will have begun the lifelong process of improving it and keeping it or another one. The following ideas may help:

1. Read professional or trade journals that specifically cover your career area.
2. Join pertinent professional associations, but not so many that you are unable to be an active, participating and dependable member.
3. Ask for ongoing job-training and upgrading. If necessary, get some on your own. Many good seminars are available at reasonable costs and computer-based education, video lessons and audiotapes are good sources.
4. Read national news magazines and books by authors with specialties in forecasting, business or careers. They will contain trends and predictions that may help you know when to anticipate a job shift.
5. Attend company management and employee club meetings and training sessions.

No one can ever be fully prepared and ahead of the job game. Even in smooth-running times, quirks occur in the economy that ripple into job change and job competition.

But by being forward looking, your chances for a happy, productive career are greatly increased. Remember: what goes around comes around. Don't get caught in the job market's revolving door.

APPENDIX A
OCCUPATIONAL PROFILES

WHERE THE JOBS ARE

The following table provides a shorthand profile of each
job title covered in the chapter listings, which included
many new jobs plus those existing occupations expected to
experience either average or rapid growth. In addition, the
table includes profiles for hundreds of jobs which are not
expected to experience significant growth.

Thus, the table provides a quick glimpse at the world
of work as it's projected through 1990. The key provided
below, along with a few explanatory comments, should en-
able you to locate and interpret the pertinent information
in each job category.

The first column, titled "Work Site," indicates the location where a particular job is likely to be performed.
Dental hygienists, for example, work in an office (O) and
blue-collar worker supervisors work in a factory (F).

"Number" is the number of employees (in thousands) expected to be needed by 1990 to meet demand in the job category. For instance, 79,000 architects will be in demand by 1990.

The salaries column lists estimated starting and mid-career salaries (in thousands of dollars) for each job title. An architect can expect to earn $14,000 the first year and reach $40,000 per year at midcareer.

The next column depicts a rate of growth—ranging from obsolence to a brand-new job—for each job category. For example, 79,000 new jobs for architects represents fast growth (F) for that job category.

The last column lists education and training requirements—ranging from on-the-job training to graduate education. Many job titles will have more than one "X" in this column, indicating that training requirements may vary depending on the degree of expertise required in a particular work environment.

Following the job listings are sample cover letters for job inquiries and requests for interviews, a sample resume and a sample thank-you letter to follow up your interview.

KEY TO COLUMN HEADINGS:

SER	Record serial number
DOT	Code from Dictionary of Occupational Titles
NR	Unallocated coding field
OCCUPATION TITLE	Self-explanatory
WORK SITE	Location of occupation
O	Office
W	Work site other than office
H	Home
F	Farm
M	Mobile (no fixed location)

NUMBER REQD	Projected number of workers required by 1990, in thousands
SALARIES	Annual salary projections in thousands of dollars
1ST	Entry level salary estimate
MID	Midcareer salary estimate
GROWTH CATEGORY	Projected growth rate of employment in the occupation
O	Obsolescent (no growth)
S	Slow growth
A	Average growth
F	Fast growth
N	New occupation
EDUCATION/TRAINING REQUIREMENTS	Education/training required for employment
O	On-the-job training
A	Apprenticeship
V	Vocational high school
2	Two-year college
4	Four-year college
G	Graduate education

SER	DOT NR	OCCUPATION TITLE	O	W	H	F	M	REQD	1ST	MID	O	S	A	F	N	O	A	V	2	4	G
124	722	A/C, Heating & Refrigeration Mechanics	X	X				207	13	19			X								X	
18	160	Accountants	X	X				1047	17	25		X									X	
532	216	Accounting Clerks	X	X																X		
162	150	Actors & Actresses	X				X	26													X	
257	020	Actuaries	X						13	30	X		X								X	
258	169	Administrative Assistants	X	X					12	28											X	
78	254	Advertising Workers	X	X				100	10	40		X		X							X	
259	002	Aeronautical Engineers	X	X					16	50	X										X	
260	013	Agricultural Engineers				X			16	40		X									X	
501	372	Air Marshalls																			X	X
164	199	Air Traffic Controllers	X	X				29	15	31	X		X		X	X	X					
120	621	Aircraft Mechanics	X	X				121	15	24		X			X	X	X					
533	193	Airline-Radio Operators																	X			
540	342	Amusement Park Vendors																	X			
460	419	Animal Breeders	X			X						X							X			
261	418	Animal Keepers	X						6	10	X					X			X			
475	419	Animal Keepers	X																			
262	041	Animal Scientists	X	X					14	26		X		X							X	
263	969	Announcers (Radio & TV)	X	X					11	35		X								X	X	
446	279	Antique Dealers	X																X	X		
264	187	Apartment House Managers	X					77	6	8		X						X				
573	187	Apartment House Managers		X														X				
127	723	Appliance Repairers		X		X			10	25	X		X							X		
265	041	Aquatic Biologists		X		X		79	19	28				X						X		
14	001	Architects	X						14	40									X	X		
452	149	Art Critics	X	X																X	X	X

SER	DOT	NR	OCCUPATION TITLE	O	W	H	F	M	REQD	1ST	MID	O	S	A	F	N	O	A	V	2	4	G
453	099		Art Teachers/Professors																		X	X
443	962		Artistic Program Assistants																			
100	709		Assemblers	X					1670	8	20	X										
574	199		Assessors																	X		
266	153		Athletic Coaches	X						15	25	X										
596	099		Athletics Directors																	X		
15	110		Attorneys	X				X	487	21	60	X										
267	294		Auctioneers					X		6	10									X		
545	294		Auctioneers																	X		
268	078		Audiologists	X						15	27			X							X	
269	807		Auto Body Repairers	X						8	15				X						X	
270	273		Auto Parts Salespersons	X						6	10				X						X	
419	213		Auto. Office Data Mgmt Analysts & Supervisors	X					250	16	25										X	
415	189		Auto. Office Info Management Directors	X					150	22	50											X
417	169		Auto. Office Quality/Production Analysts	X					100	14	22										X	
414	189		Auto. Office Rcds, Data, Info Security Managers	X					260	18	25										X	
412	189		Auto. Office Terminal/Msg Ctr Mgrs (Corp. Ofc)	X					500	18	37										X	
411	189		Auto. Office Terminal/Msg Ctr Mgrs (Single Ofc)	X					300	16	21										X	
416	161		Auto. Office Work Station Analysts	X					240	18	25										X	
117	620		Automotive Mechanics	X					1197	9	14						X					
158	315		Bakers	X					133	9	17					X	X					
579	160		Bank Auditors																		X	X

SER	DOT	NR	OCCUPATION TITLE	O	W	H	F	M	REQD	1ST	MID	O	S	A	F	N	O	A	V	2	4	G
21	186		Bank Officers & Administrators	X					643	16	29							X		X	X	X
22	211		Bank Tellers	X					531	8	12				X	X	X	X	X	X	X	
557	330		Barbers																			
157	312		Bartenders	X					382	10	31			X		X						
118	638		Battery Technicians—Fuel Cells	X					25	9	14				X	X		X				
558	332		Beauticians																	X		
553	324		Bellhops															X				
271	041		Biologists	X						12	35	X									X	
4	019		Biomedical Engineers	X					4	18	28		X									
272	019		Biomedical Technicians	X						13	25		X							X		
377	019		Bionic Electronic Technician	X					90	11	19									X		
516	609		Bit Sharpeners															X	X			
119	183		Blue Collar Worker Supervisors	X					1300	16	19		X			X		X	X			
273	623		Boatbuilders	X						10	18	X					X	X				
108	599		Boiler Tenders	X					62	11	24	X					X	X		X		
510	019		Boilerhouse Mechanics																X			
274	805		Boilermakers	X						14	22		X			X		X				
517	979		Book Trimmers																			
23	210		Bookkeepers	X	X				1904	10	17			X		X		X	X			
275	210		Bookkeeping Machine Operators	X						8	14		X					X	X			
276	041		Botanists							12	30	X								X		
491	349		Bouncers	X														X				
435	260		Brain Food Store Operators	X				X	168	16	31										
138	861		Bricklayers & Stonemasons						17	12	14		X			X		X				
121	969		Broadcast Technicians	X									X			X		X				
534	251		Brokerage Clerks																	X		

142

SER	DOT NR	OCCUPATION TITLE	O	W	H	F	M	REQD	1ST	MID	O	S	A	F	N	O	A	V	2	4	G
170	913	Bus Drivers					X	127	10	22		X				X	X	X		X	X
424	199	Business Occupations Forecasters		X				75	17	30							X	X		X	X
548	269	Buyers																			
69	162	Buyers (Wholesale & Retail)	X	X				190	17	31		X				X	X		X	X	X
544	269	Buyers Assistants																X		X		
395	199	CAD Engineering Software Specialists		X				360	19	30							X	X			
394	209	CAD Information Retrieval & Reproduction Clerks		X				300	10	12								X			
389	699	CAD Product Design Technicians		X				190	15	28							X		X		
391	199	CAD Product or Systems Inspectors		X				280	12	22							X		X		
388	017	CAD Terminal Draftsmen		X				300	14	25							X		X		
392	169	CAD Terminal Parts Cataloguers		X				125	11	18							X		X		
393	019	CAD Terminal Product Testing Engineers		X				600	14	35										X	
398	279	CAD Trng & Ed Materials Salespeople		X				95	12	20							X		X		
397	097	CAD Voc'l Trng & Ed Simulation Instructors		X				300	14	22											
396	199	CAD Voc'l Trng & Ed Simulation Software Splsts		X				150	14	19							X		X		
384	979	CAG Layout Artists		X				40	10	18							X		X		
387	169	CAG Operations Supervisors		X				20	15	25							X		X		
386	259	CAG Sales Representatives		X			X	30	15	30							X		X		
385	979	CAG Terminal Input Artists		X				40	17	18							X		X		
403	199	CAM Holographic Inspectors		X				135	12	21							X		X		

SER	DOT	NR	OCCUPATION TITLE	O	W	H	F	M	REQD	1ST	MID	O	S	A	F	N	O	A	V	2	4	G
400	699		CAM Machine & Mfg Materials Setup Mechanics	X					300	12	20								X			
406	199		CAM Mfg Matl/Finished Parts Traffic Controllers		X				20	12	14									X		
402	699		CAM Production Schedulers/Progress Controllers	X					90	12	18								X			
404	183		CAM Production Superintendents	X	X				90	15	25								X			
407	229		CAM Rcds Supervisors-Inventory, Stocking, Shipping	X	X				14	12	14								X			
401	019		CAM Special Tooling Design Engineers	X					170	14	19								X			
399	019		CAM Technicians	X	X				75	16	22											
405	199		CAM-CAD Software Coordinators	X	X				80	17	25								X			
277	660		Cabinetmakers	X						10	21		X						X			
115	822		Cable TV Installers					X	300	11	13			X	X				X			
554	341		Caddies																X			
279	078		Cardiopulmonary Technologists	X				X		9	25			X	X	X			X			
137	860		Carpenters					X	1185	16	28			X	X	X						
520	683		Carpet Weavers																X			
280	018		Cartographers	X				X		14	24		X									X
45	211		Cashiers	X				X	1554	12	17		X					X	X			
281	310		Caterers				X	X		6	10			X								
282	869		Cement Masons	X				X		10	22		X					X	X			
11	008		Chemical Engineers	X				X	55	22	33		X					X	X	X		
283	022		Chemical Laboratory Technicians	X						9	17		X						X			

SER	DOT	NR	OCCUPATION TITLE	O	W	H	F	M	REQD	1ST	MID	O	S	A	F	N	O	A	V	2	4	G
521	559		Chemical Operators		X				128	20	35			X						X		
1	022		Chemists			X			431	8	10			X								X	
178	309		Child Care Workers (Household)			X																
177	195		Child Welfare Workers (Not household)		X				432	15	21			X					X			X	
541	342		Cigarette Vendors	X																			
168	188		City Managers	X					4	33	49			X					X			X	
5	005		Civil Engineers	X					180	20	27			X								X	
284	120		Clergy Members	X						12	25			X								X	
522	689		Cloth Graders		X								X										X
285	299		Collection Clerks	X						7	13		X								X		
441	150		Comedians	X										X					X				
425	199		Commerce Occupations Forecasters		X				60	16	29								X			X	
166	310		Commercial Airline Flight Attendants					X	56	11	21			X		X	X	X	X			
165	196		Commercial Airline Pilots					X	82	31	67											X	
86	650		Compositors & Typesetters		X				128	18	22											X	
67	078		Computer Axial Tomography Technologists						25	12	20	X				X	X	X	X			
93	219		Computer Console & Equipment Operators	X	X				558	10	18			X		X	X	X	X			
382	017		Computer Drafting Technicians		X				300	18	30								X			
381	979		Computer Graphics Technicians		X				150	20	35								X			

145

SER	DOT NR	OCCUPATION TITLE	O	W	H	F	M	REQD	1ST	MID	O	S	A	F	N	O	A	V	2	4	G
92	119	Computer Manufacturing Inspectors	X					250	17	32			X		X		X	X	X		
383	199	Computer Modeling & Simulation Technicians		X				300	25	40									X		
90	199	Computer Programmers	X	X	X			258	19	27			X	X			X	X	X		
91	726	Computer Service Technicians		X	X		X	93	18	28			X	X			X	X	X		
421	199	Computer Software Writers—General	X		X			1830	20	30			X								
89	199	Computer Systems Analysts	X	X				260	20	26			X	X			X	X	X		
205	239	Computer Terminal Distributive Info Processors						140	20	35								X	X		
200	239	Computer Terminal Information Processors						270	20	30					X				X		
145	869	Construction Laborers & Carpenter Helpers					X	851	13	24			X		X						
506	869	Construction Workers																X		X	X
561	199	Convention Planners																			
286	139	Copywriters	X					103	8	28		X								X	X
175	379	Correctional Institution Officers	X						12	25			X	X	X		X	X	X		
571	195	Counselors	X					350	8	15		X			X					X	X
44	238	Counter Clerks		X	X				12	19			X	X							
287	209	Court Reporters		X	X			148	12	17		X	X	X	X		X	X	X		
112	921	Crane, Derrick & Hoist Operators		X	X							X	X	X			X	X			
288	241	Credit Investigators	X						7	12			X	X				X	X		
575	199	Credit Officers											X	X				X	X		

SER	DOT NR	OCCUPATION TITLE	O	W	H	F	M	REQD	1ST	MID	O	S	A	F	N	O	A	V	2	4	G
502	379	Customs Officers		X																X	X
465	078	Cytotechnologists		X															X		X
163	151	Dancers					X	30									X	X			
289	976	Darkroom Laboratory Technicians		X					7	15		X					X				
290	079	Dental Assistants	X	X					8	12				X			X			X	
48	079	Dental Hygienists	X					36	11	14			X				X			X	
49	078	Dental Laboratory Technicians		X				53	17	30				X	X		X				
47	072	Dentists	X	X				140	22	55		X		X			X				X
542	290	Department Store Sales Clerks															X		X		
523	639	Diesel Engine Testers																			
291	631	Diesel Mechanics		X			X		10	23			X	X			X			X	
292	078	Dietetic Technicians		X					13	24			X	X			X			X	
61	077	Dieticians		X				59	16	26				X			X				
293	969	Disc Jockeys		X					9	28		X			X		X	X			
294	318	Dishwashers		X					6	7				X		X	X				
507	239	Dispatchers															X				
295	199	Divers					X														
296	359	Dog Groomers		X					7	14		X					X				
476	418	Dog Groomers										X					X	X			
447	017	Drafters																X			
149	785	Dressmakers & Seamstresses (Non-factory)			X			107	10	24		X				X					
518	606	Drill Press Operators															X				
146	849	Drywall Installers & Finishers					X		84	18	28			X			X				
426	199	Economic Occupations Forecasters		X				45	14	19										X	

SER	DOT NR	OCCUPATION TITLE	O	W	H	F	M	REQD	1ST	MID	O	S	A	F	N	O	A	V	2	4	G
19	050	Economists	X					44	14	25			X							X	X
454	132	Editorial Writers		X	X								X							X	X
83	139	Editors, Writers & Reporters		X				167	12	50			X							X	
428	199	Educational Institutions Occupations F'casters		X				20	12	20			X							X	
113	821	Electric Power Line & Cable Maint. Mechanics					X	120	12	18			X		X						
6	003	Electrical & Electronic Engineers					X	357	22	33			X							X	
511	019	Electrical Technologists	X	X									X						X		
130	828	Electrical/Electronic Engineering Technicians	X	X				359	12	24			X		X		X	X			
466	829	Electricians											X						X		
132	824	Electricians (Construction)					X	648	20	31			X		X		X	X			
65	078	Electrocardiogram Technicians					X	20	11	18		X		X	X			X			
66	078	Electroencephalographic Technicians					X	5	12	20		X		X	X			X			
420	239	Electronic Mail Operations Specialists	X					300	12	16			X								
56	078	Emergency Medical Technicians						120	10	23			X		X		X	X			
116	959	Energy Auditors					X	150	12	16					X	X					
134	952	Energy Conservation Technicians		X				1500	13	26					X						
131	828	Engineering & Science Technicians		X				885	10	22			X					X			
297	019	Engineering Aides	X	X					10	18			X		X						
129	979	Engineering Draftsmen	X					335	10	22	X				X		X	X			

148

SER	DOT NR	OCCUPATION TITLE	O	W	H	F	M	REQD	1ST	MID	O	S	A	F	N	O	A	V	2	4	C
470	199	Environmental Analysts		X																	X	X
434	261	Erotic Boutique Owners	X	X																	X	X
82	168	Estimators & Investigators						534	11	17	X				X					X		
144	850	Excavating, Grading & Road Machine Operators					X	456	20	30	X				X			X				
503	375	FBI Special Agents																			X	X
186	409	Farm Laborers (Wage Workers)				X		895	7		X											X
477	409	Farm Workers										X					X					
185	409	Farm Workers & Supervisors				X		1218	13	22	X	X				X						
184	409	Farmers & Farm Managers				X		1485			X	X				X						
455	142	Fashion Designers											X								X	X
508	197	Ferryboat Operators																			X	X
46	206	File Clerks	X	X				324	8	14	X											
524	976	Film Processing Supervisors																				
538	199	Financial Aid Counselors																				
497	379	Fire Inspectors																	X		X	X
496	379	Fire Wardens																X	X		X	X
172	373	Firefighters					X	14	20					X				X				
498	379	Fish and Game Wardens									X							X				
278	197	Fishing Vessel Captains					X	12	21				X					X				
559	352	Flight Attendants			X			9	19				X									
181	149	Floral Designers			X			56			X						X	X				
528	260	Food Clerks											X									
159	310	Food Counter Workers	X	X				426	7	14			X	X		X	X	X				
156	319	Food Service Workers (Commercial cooks)	X	X				4436	7	20			X	X		X	X	X				
152	529	Food Technologists	X	X				15	18	30		X										
298	452	Foresters	X	X				13	20			X						X	X			

SER	DOT	NR	OCCUPATION TITLE	O	W	H	F	M	REQD	1ST	MID	O	S	A	F	N	O	A	V	2	4	G
486	452		Foresters																			
482	459		Foresters Aides																X	X	X	X
111	922		Fork Lift & Tow Motor Operators		X				366	8	13		X						X			
182	922		Freight & Materials Handlers		X				722	10	24		X						X			
549	199		Fund Raisers																	X		
560	338		Funeral Attendants															X		X		
299	187		Funeral Directors	X	X					12	28		X							X		
576	199		Funeral Directors															X		X		
487	412		Gamekeepers																		X	X
183	406		Gardeners & Groundskeepers (Non-farm)		X			X	601	6	21		X								X	X
376	019		Genetic Engineering Technicians		X				250	20	30										X	
7	019		Genetic Engineers		X				150	23	38					X					X	X
471	029		Geographers													X					X	X
2	024		Geologists		X				34	20	28			X							X	
12	029		Geophysicists		X				12	20	28			X				X			X	
378	078		Geriatric Social Technicians		X				300	12	18										X	
180	079		Geriatric Social Workers		X	X			450	15	21					X				X		
379	078		Gerontological Science Aides		X				300	12	18						X					
300	865		Glaziers					X				X	X									
591	153		Golf Professionals							8	12							X		X		
448	141		Graphic Illustrators															X		X		
492	372		Guards																X			
176	332		Hairdressers & Cosmetologists	X	X				565	7	14		X						X	X		
380	078		Handicapped Compensating Techs Diagnosticians		X				80	13	17					X		X			X	

SER	DOT NR	OCCUPATION TITLE	O	W	H	F	M	REQD	1ST	MID	O	S	A	F	N	O	A	V	2	4	G
136	955	Hazardous Waste Disposal Technicians	X				X	1500	15	28					X			X	X	X	X
472	079	Health Educators											X							X	X
55	169	Health Service Administrators	X					220	19	50					X	X					
109	639	Heavy Equipment Mechanics					X	963	12	17				X	X					X	X
456	149	Historic Restorers																X		X	X
97	168	Holographic Inspectors						200	18	20									X		
123	828	Home Electronic Interactive Systems Technicians				X	X	200	15	21	X				X	X					
418	828	Home/Office Interactive Work System Technicians	X				X	180	14	20								X			
478	418	Horse Exercisers																	X		
479	418	Horseshoers (Blacksmiths)																	X		
301	409	Horticulturists	X	X					10	26							X	X			
564	355	Hospital Orderlies	X									X									
304	187	Hotel Sales Managers	X	X					12	20		X	X	X						X	
302	249	Hotel/Motel Clerks	X	X					6	12		X	X	X			X	X			
303	187	Hotel/Motel Managers	X	X					13	25		X	X	X		X	X			X	
179	301	Housecleaners & Servants			X			491	7	14					X						
135	869	Housing Rehabilitation Technicians			X	X		1750	14	24					X	X					
305	141	Illustrators/Commercial Artists	X						9	18		X		X				X			
306	142	Industrial Designers	X					245	10	21									X	X	X
8	012	Industrial Engineers	X						22	30		X		X				X		X	X
375	078	Industrial Hygiene Technicians	X					70	12	16					X	X			X	X	X
106	819	Industrial Laser Process Technicians	X					600	30	50											

151

SER	DOT NR	OCCUPATION TITLE	O	W	H	F	M	REQD	1ST	MID	O	S	A	F	N	O	A	V	2	4	G
110	639	Industrial Machine Repairers		X				507	16	27			X								X
423	199	Industrial Occupations		X				80	17	25										X	
431	199	Industrial Relations Occupations Forecasters		X				50	14	25										X	
193	199	Industrial Robot Production Technicians						800	15	24							X		X		
467	383	Insect Pest Controllers															X				
461	716	Instrument Repairers															X		X		
73	250	Insurance Agents, Brokers & Underwriters	X					532	14	40		X			X					X	
307	142	Interior Designers		X			X		8	22		X							X		
308	137	Interpreters	X				X		9	24		X								X	
493	372	Jailers	X																		
309	382	Janitors/Custodians		X					7	13			X				X				
310	700	Jewelers		X					14	20			X				X				
588	153	Jockeys														X					
88	199	Key Punch Operators	X					200	15	21		X			X		X				
462	199	Laboratory Assistants											X				X				
311	001	Landscape Architects		X			X		17	28			X				X			X	
488	019	Landscape Contractors																		X	X
483	019	Landscape Workers																X			
312	019	Laser Electric Optics Technicians		X					9	22		X					X		X		
148	369	Laundry Operators & Dry Cleaners		X				203	10	13		X			X						
580	249	Law Clerks		X																X	X

SER	DOT NR	OCCUPATION TITLE	O	W	H	F	M	REQD	1ST	MID	O	S	A	F	N	O	A	V	2	4	G
449	142	Layout Designers		X															X		
546	299	Leasing Agents																	X		
313	201	Legal Secretaries	X						8	18							X			X	
33	109	Librarians, Historians & Curators		X				199	14	27				X						X	
567	079	Licensed Practical Nurses																X	X		
494	349	Lifeguards																X	X		
85	972	Lithographers		X				45	27	38		X					X		X		
84	659	Lithographic Press Operators		X				81	14	17			X				X				
314	709	Locksmiths		X			X		6	18		X									
480	454	Loggers					X						X				X				
103	609	Machine Operators		X				736	11	33		X				X					
96	609	Machinists & Job Set-up Workers		X				658	20	35		X	X				X				
40	230	Mail Carriers		X			X	250	19	21	X	X				X					
104	168	Manufacturing Inspectors		X				336	12	22		X						X			
315	349	Marina Workers		X					8	13		X						X			
316	014	Marine Engineers		X					21	36		X						X		X	
317	019	Marine Surveyors		X			X		8	14		X								X	
318	199	Market Research Analysts	X						15	28			X							X	
319	334	Masseurs/Masseuses		X					23	27			X				X				
95	909	Materials Utilization Technicians		X				400	15	24					X					X	
581	020	Mathematicians																	X	X	
154	316	Meat Cutters & Butchers				X		190	12	24	X	X								X	
512	017	Mechanical Drafters (Not plant)																			
9	007	Mechanical Engineers		X				237	20	28				X						X	

153

SER	DOT	NR	OCCUPATION TITLE	O	W	H	F	M	REQD	1ST	MID	O	S	A	F	N	O	A	V	2	4	G
513	019		Mechanical Technologists																	X		
582	199		Media Specialists																	X	X	X
457	141		Medical Illustrators																		X	X
62	078		Medical Laboratory Technicians			X			205	12	21			X						X		
320	245		Medical Office Assistants	X						7	14		X							X	X	X
63	219		Medical Records Technicians			X			20	12	23			X			X			X	X	X
321	201		Medical Secretaries	X						7	18		X					X		X		
473	011		Metallurgists																			
322	025		Meteorologists			X				16	31		X							X	X	X
323	041		Microbiologists			X				12	35			X			X			X		X
94	729		Microcomputer Diagnosticians	X		X			200	20	35					X	X	X	X	X	X	
60	079		Midwives				X		15	10	20					X	X	X				
430	199		Military Occupations Forecasters			X			15	12	20			X								X
324	899		Millwrights					X		10	20	X					X					
325	299		Models			X				12	14		X						X		X	X
326	620		Motorcycle Repairers			X				10	16		X						X		X	X
583	199		Museum Curators																			
458	142		Museum Display Artists																			
161	152		Musicians			X			138	14	28									X	X	X
442	152		Musicians																			
504	375		Narcotics Agents														X			X		
519	699		New Car Inspectors																			
327	015		Nuclear Engineers			X				16	28		X				X			X		
328	078		Nuclear Medical Technicians			X				13	18		X				X					
489	180		Nursery Managers																X			
563	099		Nursery School Attendants													X	X			X	X	X

SER	DOT NR	OCCUPATION TITLE	O	W	H	F	M	REQD	1ST	MID	O	S	A	F	N	O	A	V	2	4	G
329	079	Nurses Aides	X						6	12			X					X			X
572	079	Nursing Supervisors																		X	X
330	076	Occupational Therapists		X					15	22		X									
568	076	Occupational Therapy Assistants																	X		
331	029	Oceanographers	X	X			X		12	17	X									X	
529	249	Office Clerks															X	X			
128	822	Office Communications Equipment Installers		X			X	25	13	29	X						X	X			
413	209	Office Info Center Terminal Operators	X	X				600	14	23	X						X		X		
125	733	Office Machine Repairers	X	X			X	55	10	14		X			X			X			
332	729	Office Machine Servicers	X	X			X		8	15			X	X				X			
333	189	Office Managers	X						11	16		X								X	
535	189	Office Supervisors														X	X		X		
107	869	Operating Engineers (Construction Machinery)	X	X				190	21	28		X					X	X		X	
334	079	Optometrists	X	X					20	38		X									X
463	355	Orderlies	X	X											X			X			
335	079	Orthodontists	X	X			X		12	28		X			X			X			
336	623	Outboard Motor Mechanics	X	X			X		7	16					X	X					
155	529	Packers & Wrappers (Not meat or produce)	X	X			X	600	9	14	X	X					X				
555	353	Pages/Ushers														X		X			
139	849	Painters & Paperhangers	X				X	463	15	29				X	X						
141	749	Painters—Automotive	X	X			X	41	18	28	X				X						
140	840	Painters—Construction & Maintenance	X	X			X	469	16	24				X	X						

SER	DOT NR	OCCUPATION TITLE	O	W	H	F	M	REQD	1ST	MID	O	S	A	F	N	O	A	V	2	4	G
142	749	Painters—Manufactured Goods	X	X				181	13	26	X											X
337	970	Painters, Sign	X	X			X		7	15								X	X		X	
338	119	Paralegal Assistants	X				X		9	16		X	X									
577	119	Paralegals	X																X	X	X	
468	079	Paramedics																		X	X	
339	159	Park Rangers	X				X		11	22	X	X									X	
340	195	Parole Officers	X						9	16	X	X									X	
101	693	Patternmakers	X	X				4	18	29	X	X					X					
20	166	Personnel & Labor Relations Workers	X	X				93	15	29	X		X				X				X	
17	166	Personnel Administrators	X	X				405	28	50	X			X				X			X	
341	383	Pest Control Workers					X		7	12		X	X						X		X	
50	074	Pharmacists	X	X				141	21	24				X							X	
343	971	Photoengravers	X	X					10	12	X	X					X				X	
188	143	Photographers	X	X	X		X	91	14	21	X	X			X		X				X	
464	976	Photographic Laboratory Workers	X													X		X			X	
344	976	Photographic Process Workers	X						7	12	X						X				X	
57	076	Physical Therapists	X					34	17	27	X						X				X	
565	079	Physical Therapy Aides											X				X				X	
345	079	Physical Therapy Assistants	X						8	16			X					X	X			
58	079	Physician Assistants	X	X				10	18	22	X		X					X	X			
51	079	Physicians & Osteopaths	X	X				424	38	74	X							X	X			X
3	023	Physicists	X					44	15	22							X				X	
509	801	Pipe Fitters															X					
556	353	Plant Guides															X					
515	183	Plant Managers																X		X	X	X

SER	DOT NR	OCCUPATION TITLE	O	W	H	F	M	REQD	1ST	MID	O	S	A	F	N	O	A	V	2	4	G
490	409	Plant Propagators						24	19	28										X	X
147	842	Plasterers		X			X	478	15	30		X		X				X	X		
143	862	Plumbers & Pipefitters					X	12	22	50		X		X				X	X		X
52	070	Podiatrists	X		X																X	X
505	188	Police Chiefs																	X		
499	375	Police Inspectors														X			X		
500	375	Police Officers														X			X		
174	375	Policemen & Detectives	X	X				512	15	28		X			X				X	X	
10	051	Political Scientists	X		X			15	15	22	X							X	X	X	
64	078	Positron Emission Technologists			X			25	12	20					X	X		X	X	X	X
38	230	Postal Clerks		X				285	18	21	X		X		X		X				
444	144	Pottery Workers																X			
484	411	Poultry Breeders			X							X						X	X		
54	079	Practical Nurses						550	9	12	X	X						X	X	X	
87	651	Printing Press Operators		X				178	17	23							X				
459	149	Producers		X				5	20	75								X	X	X	X
167	153	Professional Athletes																	X		X
569	079	Psychiatric Aides																	X		
346	045	Psychologists, Clinical		X					24	40		X									X
347	045	Psychologists, Counseling		X					12	22			X								X
16	165	Public Relations Managers	X					131	12	32	X								X	X	X
584	199	Public Relations Specialists													O					X	X
102	619	Punch Press & Stamping Operators		X				183	20	31	X				X						
70	162	Purchasing Agents & Buyers (not Whls/Retail)	X	X				244	16	31	X		X		X			X	X	X	
348	199	Quality Control Inspectors		X					7	16	X		X					X			

157

SER	DOT NR	OCCUPATION TITLE	O	W	H	F	M	REQD	1ST	MID	O	S	A	F	N	O	A	V	2	4	G
122	720	Radio & TV Mechanics		X	X			120	11	19				X			X	X	X	X	X
68	078	Radiologic (X-ray) Technologists			X			106	14	19	X								X		
74	250	Real Estate Agents & Brokers	X		X			582	13	29				X		X	X		X		
349	191	Real Estate Appraisers		X			X		13	18	X			X		X					
35	237	Receptionists	X		X			635	8	12								X	X		
351	194	Recording Engineers		X					7	14							X		X		
589	159	Recreation Aides								14							X		X		
34	159	Recreation Workers		X	X			135	12	17		X	X	X		X			X		X
53	075	Registered Nurses	X	X	X			1302	14	20		X	X	X		X			X		X
539	249	Registrars															X	X		X	X
32	099	Rehabilitation Counselors						25	13	18			X			X					
59	076	Respiratory Therapists		X				50	14	18		X	X			X		X	X		
352	187	Restaurant Managers		X					14	35		X	X				X	X			
196	199	Robot Installation & Operations Technicians						250	12	22											
408	199	Robot On-the-Job Programmers		X				200	12	20								X			
198	199	Robot Repairmen						140	14	22								X			
13	019	Robotic Engineers		X				500	23	35					X				X		
409	699	Robots—Programmed Tool Handlers		X				100	12	18							X	X			
353	843	Roofers				X			8	17	X				X						
514	189	Safety Inspectors									X			X					X		
354	911	Sailors				X			15	22	X			X							
75	251	Sales Agents—Stocks & Bonds	X				X	67	11	50			X		X	X					
80	290	Sales Clerks—Retail		X				2345	6	14	X			X		X				X		

SER	DOT NR	OCCUPATION TITLE	O	W	H	F	M	REQD	1ST	MID	O	S	A	F	N	O	A	V	2	4	G
71	163	Sales Managers	X	X				705	12	45			X					X	X	X	X
76	279	Sales Representatives—Manufacturing	X	X				440	16	37			X					X	X	X	X
77	269	Sales Representatives—Wholesale	X	X				1001	18	33			X					X		X	
550	273	Sales Representatives for Aircraft Equipment												X						X	X
552	259	Sales Representatives For Psychological Tests												X						X	X
551	271	Sales Reps For Copying Machines/Computers												X						X	X
79	269	Sales Workers—Retail	X	X	X			3300	7	14	X							X			
81	259	Sales Workers—Services & Construction	X	X				222	7	17	X							X			
72	299	Salespersons & Peddlers	X	X				178	8	12	X							X		X	
356	199	Sanitary Inspectors	X				X		8	16	X							X		X	
525	454	Sawmill Supervisors																	X		
25	099	School Administrators						431	23	43		X								X	
469	199	Science Laboratory Technicians																	X		
590	159	Scorekeepers																X			
36	209	Secretaries & Stenographers	X	X				3940	9	12							X	X	X		
495	239	Security Dispatchers															X	X			
173	372	Security Guards	X	X			X	548	12	18			X			X	X	X			
126	620	Service Station Mechanics & Attendants		X				33	8	12	X		X			X	X	X	X		
150	789	Sewers & Stitchers	X					788	9	16						X		X		X	
99	619	Sheet Metal Workers	X					161	18	28			X				X				
41	222	Shipping & Receiving Clerks	X					505	8	18						X		X			

SER	DOT NR	OCCUPATION TITLE	O	W	H	F	M	REQD	1ST	MID	O	S	A	F	N	O	A	V	2	4	G
445	152	Singers	X					480	10	26			X					X		X	
31	195	Social & Recreational Workers											X						X	X	
566	195	Social Case Aides																X		X	X
570	195	Social Case Workers																		X	X
562	195	Social Directors																			
357	019	Solar Energy Technicians	X				X		14	20								X			
358	079	Speech Pathologists	X						19	25		X								X	X
585	131	Speech Writers																			
592	099	Sports Instructors																	X		
450	159	Stage Set Designers																	X		
42	216	Statistical Clerks	X		X			387	7	12		X	X						X		
359	020	Statisticians		X					15	29		X	X							X	
43	222	Stock Clerks & Storekeepers	X					533	8	18		X			X						
153	525	Stock Handlers				X		941	8	12		X			X						
578	372	Store Detectives	X																X		
360	809	Structural Steel Workers	X				X		15	19		X					X				
593	159	Stunt Performers																	X		
526	559	Supervisors of Chemical Production																		X	X
527	729	Supervisors of Electronic-Computer Assembly											X							X	X
474	070	Surgeons																			X
361	078	Surgical Technicians	X			X			8	16								X			
536	199	Survey Workers																	X		
362	018	Surveyors					X		9	24		X	X								
363	785	Tailors	X						6	14		X						X		X	
586	110	Tax Lawyers										X								X	X

SER	DOT NR	OCCUPATION TITLE	O	W	H	F	M	REQD	1ST	MID	O	S	A	F	N	O	A	V	2	4	G
451	149	Taxidermists		X																X		
364	099	Teacher Aides		X					7	9								X			
26	090	Teachers—College & University						691	23	31		X					X		X		X	X
27	092	Teachers—Elementary School		X				1600	17			X									X	
28	092	Teachers—Kindergarten		X				243	17			X									X	
597	099	Teachers—Physical Education											X								X	X
366	092	Teachers—Pre-school		X					10	16		X									X	
29	091	Teachers—Secondary School		X				1243	18	16			X								X	
365	094	Teachers—Special Needs		X					14	16		X									X	
530	239	Telegraph Clerks																X	X			
189	254	Telemarketing Advertising & Scenario Writers						110	18	35					X	X	X	X			X	
191	829	Telemarketing Audio-Visual Technicians						50	25	40					X	X	X	X			X	
194	199	Telemarketing Computer Programmers						60	20	35					X		X	X				
195	299	Telemarketing Sales—Ship/Billg Clerks/Supers						50	8	18					X	X	X	X				
190	163	Telemarketing Sales Program Supervisors						65	25	100					X	X	X	X			X	
192	254	Telemarketing Splsts—Recdg/Cust Order Take-off						80	15	30					X	X	X	X				
114	822	Telephone Installers & Repairers					X	309	10	12				X	X		X	X				
39	235	Telephone Operators	X					316	8	10		X			X	X						
206	019	Teletext Broadcast Communications Engineers						40	20	40											X	

SER	DOT NR	OCCUPATION TITLE	O	W	H	F	M	REQD	1ST	MID	O	S	A	F	N	O	A	V	2	4	G
197	139	Teletext Computer Splsts—Compsn, Format, Editg						65	16	40					X					X	X
207	259	Teletext Interactive Correspondent						30	18	25					X	X	X				X
203	199	Teletext Operations Supervisors						25	20	34						X	X	X			
208	163	Teletext Senior Editors & Directors						25	30	50					X	X				X	X
201	254	Teletext Specialists—Marketing			X			30	18	40					X	X		X		X	X
202	199	Teletext Specialists—Software Programming			X			30	18	30					X	X		X			
199	254	Teletext Splsts—CATV Liaison & Scheduling						30	17	38					X	X		X			X
204	219	Teletext Supervsrs—Library, Research, Copy, Dist						20	20	30					X	X		X			X
531	251	Tellers																			
594	153	Tennis Professionals																X	X		
151	689	Textile Machine Operators				X		323	9	17		X			X	X	X				
547	269	Tobacco Buyers										X	X							X		
98	601	Tool & Die Makers				X		178	21	37		X					X		X		
367	209	Transcribing Machine Operators	X						8	12				X			X				
187	919	Travel Agents	X					52	10	18				X	X	X	X	X			X
537	359	Travel Guides																X	X	X	
481	454	Tree Cutters																X		X	
485	451	Tree Surgeons																X	X		
171	909	Truck Drivers					X	2275	17	27					X	X		X		X	
433	405	Truffle Farmers					X											X			

SER	DOT	NR	OCCUPATION TITLE	O	W	H	F	M	REQD	1ST	MID	O	S	A	F	N	O	A	V	2	4	G
37	203		Typists	X	X				1023	8	12			X					X			X
595	153		Umpires																X	X		
368	780		Upholsterers		X										X						X	
24	199		Urban & Regional Planners	X					31	12	17		X									
427	199		Urban Planners Occupations Forecasters		X				20	19	35										X	
369	073		Veterinarians		X		X	X		14	57			X								
370	079		Veterinary Assistants		X		X	X		6	12			X						X		
30	097		Vocational & Educational Counselors		X				53	14	26				X						X	
429	199		Vocational Counseling/Trng Occupatns F'casters		X				20	12	20										X	X
587	097		Vocational Educators		X					7	12											
160	311		Waiters & Waitresses		X				1700	6	12			X		X						
371	245		Ward Clerks, Hospital		X					12	12			X				X				
133	955		Waste & Water Treatment Plant Operators		X				41	12	14			X		X		X	X		X	
543	359		Wedding Consultants		X							X							X			
105	819		Welders & Cutters	X					692	22	28		X				X					
372	203		Word Processing Operators		X					7	13	X	X	X				X				
373	099		Youth Counselors		X					8	15			X								
374	049		Zoologists		X					12	25	X	X						X		X	
209	00	1	OCCUPATIONS IN ARCHITECTURE & ENGINEERING																			
14	001		Architects	X	X	X			79	14	40			X	X						X	X
311	001		Landscape Architects	X	X					17	28			X							X	X
259	002		Aeronautical Engineers	X	X		X			16	50		X								X	X

SER	DOT NR	OCCUPATION TITLE	O	W	H	F	M	REQD	1ST	MID	O	S	A	F	N	O	A	V	2	4	G
6	003	Electrical & Electronic Engineers	X					357	22	33											X
5	005	Civil Engineers	X					180	20	27				X						X	
9	007	Mechanical Engineers	X					237	20	28				X						X	
11	008	Chemical Engineers	X					55	22	33			X							X	
473	011	Metallurgists	X										X								
8	012	Industrial Engineers	X					245	22	30				X							
260	013	Agricultural Engineers				X			16	40		X									
316	014	Marine Engineers							21	36		X									
327	015	Nuclear Engineers							16	28			X								
388	017	CAD Terminal Draftsmen	X					300	14	25							X	X			
382	017	Computer Drafting Technicians	X					300	18	30									X	X	
447	017	Drafters																	X	X	
512	017	Mechanical Drafters																	X	X	
280	018	Cartographers	X				X		14	24										X	
362	018	Surveyors	X				X		9	24										X	
4	019	Biomedical Engineers	X					4	18	28									X		X
272	019	Biomedical Technicians	X					90	13	25				X					X		
377	019	Bionic Electronic Technicians	X						11	19									X		
510	019	Boilerhouse Mechanics																			
393	019	CAD Terminal Product Testing Engineers	X					600	14	35										X	
401	019	CAM Special Tooling Design Engineers	X					170	14	19							X				
399	019	CAM Technicians	X					75	16	22											
511	019	Electrical Technologists																	X		
297	019	Engineering Aides	X	X					10	18							X				

SER	DOT	NR	OCCUPATION TITLE	O	W	H	F	M	REQD	1ST	MID	O	S	A	F	N	O	A	V	2	4	G
376	019		Genetic Engineering Technicians	X					250	20	30											X
7	019		Genetic Engineers		X				150	23	38					X					X	X
488	019		Landscape Contractors																		X	X
483	019		Landscape Workers																	X		
312	019		Laser Electro Optics Technicians	X						9	22			X					X		X	
317	019		Marine Surveyors	X				X		8	14		X								X	
513	019		Mechanical Technologists	X																X		
13	019		Robotic Engineers	X				X	500	23	35					X					X	
357	019		Solar Energy Technicians	X				X		14	20								X		X	
206	019		Teletext Broadcast Communications Engineers						40	20	40					X	X				X	
210	02	1	OCCUPATIONS IN MATHEMATICS & PHYSICAL SCIENCES																			
257	020		Actuaries	X						13	30		X								X	
581	020		Mathematicians																		X	X
359	020		Statisticians	X						15	29			X							X	X
283	022		Chemical Laboratory Technicians	X						9	17			X	X					X		
1	022		Chemists	X					128	20	35			X							X	X
3	023		Physicists	X					44	15	22				X						X	X
2	024		Geologists	X					34	20	28			X							X	X
322	025		Meteorologists	X						16	31				X						X	X
471	029		Geographers	X									X									
12	029		Geophysicists	X					12	20	28		X								X	X
331	029		Oceanographers	X				X		12	17		X								X	X

SER	DOT	NR	OCCUPATION TITLE	O	W	H	F	M	REQD	1ST	MID	O	S	A	F	N	O	A	V	2	4	G
432	04	1	**OCCUPATIONS IN LIFE SCIENCES**																			
262	041		Animal Scientists	X			X			14	26			X								X	
265	041		Aquatic Biologists	X				X		19	28		X									X	
271	041		Biologists	X						12	35		X									X	
276	041		Botanists	X						12	30		X									X	
323	041		Microbiologists	X						12	35		X									X	
346	045		Psychologists, Clinical	X						24	40			X									X
347	045		Psychologists, Counseling	X						12	22				X								X
374	049		Zoologists	X						12	25		X									X	
211	05	1	**OCCUPATIONS IN SOCIAL SCIENCES**																			
19	050		Economists	X					44	14	25			X								X	
10	051		Political Scientists	X					15	15	22		X									X	
212	07	1	**OCCUPATIONS IN MEDICINE & HEALTH**																			
52	070		Podiatrists	X					12	22	50			X									X
474	070		Surgeons	X																			X
47	072		Dentists	X					140	22	55		X										X
369	073		Veterinarians		X			X		14	57		X										X
50	074		Pharmacists		X				141	21	24		X									X	
53	075		Registered Nurses	X	X				1302	14	20		X									X	
330	076		Occupational Therapists		X					15	22		X									X	
568	076.		Occupational Therapy Assistants																		X		
57	076		Physical Therapists	X					34	17	27		X									X	
59	076		Respiratory Therapists		X				50	14	18		X								X	X	

SER	DOT NR	OCCUPATION TITLE	O	W	H	F	M	REQD	1ST	MID	O	S	A	F	N	O	A	V	2	4	G
61	077	Dieticians	X	X				59	16	26			X	X					X		X	X
268	078	Audiologists	X	X					15	27		X		X				X			X	X
279	078	Cardiopulmonary Technologists	X	X					9	25					X				X	X		
67	078	Computer Axial Tomography Technologists	X					25	12	20					X	X		X	X	X		
465	078	Cytotechnologists	X					53	17	30									X			
49	078	Dental Laboratory Technicians	X						13	24			X	X	X			X				X
292	078	Dietetic Technicians	X					20	11	18			X		X			X	X			
65	078	Electrocardiogram Technicians	X					5	12	20			X	X	X			X	X			
66	078	Electroencephalographic Technicians	X						12	20			X									
56	078	Emergency Medical Technicians					X	120	10	23			X	X				X	X	X		X
378	078	Geriatric Service Technicians	X					300	12	18								X		X		
379	078	Gerontological Science Aides	X					300	12	18												
380	078	Handicapped Compensating Techs Diagnosticians	X					80	13	17									X			
375	078	Industrial Hygiene Technicians	X					70	12	16											X	
62	078	Medical Laboratory Technicians	X					205	12	21			X	X				X	X			X
328	078	Nuclear Medical Technicians	X						13	18			X	X				X	X			X
64	078	Positron Emission Technologists	X					25	12	20					X	X	X	X				X
68	078	Radiologic (X-ray) Technologists	X					106	14	19	X						X	X		X	X	X
361	078	Surgical Technicians	X										X	X				X	X			
290	079	Dental Assistants	X						8	16			X	X				X	X			
48	079	Dental Hygienists	X		X	X		36	8	12		X	X									
180	079	Geriatric Social Workers	X	X				450	11	14						X					X	
472	079	Health Educators	X	X					15	21			X	X				X			X	X

167

SER	DOT	NR	OCCUPATION TITLE	O	W	H	F	M	REQD	1ST	MID	O	S	A	F	N	O	A	V	2	4	G
567	079		Licensed Practical Nurses																			
60	079		Midwives			X			15	10	20									X		
329	079		Nurses Aides		X					6	12					X	X					X	X
572	079		Nursing Supervisors										X		X						X	X
334	079		Optometrists		X	X				20	38		X									
335	079		Orthodontists		X	X				12	28		X		X							
468	079		Paramedics															X				
565	079		Physical Therapy Aides															X			X	
345	079		Physical Therapy Assistants	X	X					8	16		X							X		
58	079		Physician Assistants	X	X				10	18	22				X					X	X	
51	079		Physicians & Osteopaths	X	X	X			424	38	74	X										X
54	079		Practical Nurses				X		550	9	12											
569	079		Psychiatric Aides										X							X	X	
358	079		Speech Pathologists	X	X					19	25		X							X	X	
370	079		Veterinary Assistants	X	X			X		6	12		X							X	X	
213	09	1	OCCUPATIONS IN EDUCATION																			
26	090		Teachers—College & University	X					691	23	31	X										X
29	091		Teachers—Secondary School	X					1243	18	16			X						X	X	
27	092		Teachers—Elementary School	X					1600	17	16		X							X	X	
28	092		Teachers—Kindergarten	X					243	17	22		X							X	X	
366	092		Teachers—Pre-school	X						10	16	X								X	X	
365	094		Teachers—Special Needs	X						14	16		X							X	X	
397	097		CAD Voc'l Trng & Ed Simulation Instructors	X					300	14	22											
30	097		Vocational & Educational Counselors	X					53	14	26		X		X					X		
587	097		Vocational Educators																	X	X	

SER	DOT	NR	OCCUPATION TITLE	O	W	H	F	M	REQD	1ST	MID	S	A	F	N	O	A	V	2	4	G
453	099		Art Teachers/Professors																	X	X
596	099		Athletics Directors																	X	X
563	099		Nursury School Attendants															X			
32	099		Rehabilitation Counselors		X				25	13	18			X	X					X	
25	099		School Administrators		X				431	23	43	X	X					X		X	
592	099		Sports Instructors															X	X		
364	099		Teacher Aides		X					7	9		X					X			
597	099		Teachers—Physical Education		X								X							X	X
373	099		Youth Counselors		X					8	15		X	X						X	
214	10	1	OCCUPATIONS IN MUSEUM, LIBRARY & ARCHIVAL SCI.																		
33	109		Librarians, Historians & Curators		X				199	14	27		X							X	
215	11	1	OCCUPATIONS IN LAW & JURISPRUDENCE																		
15	110		Attorneys	X		X			487	21	60			X	X						X
586	110		Tax Lawyers		X				250	17	32		X		X	X				X	X
92	119		Computer Manufacturing Inspectors		X											X	X	X			
338	119		Paralegal Assistants	X						9	16		X							X	
577	119		Paralegals																X		
169	12	1	OCCUPATIONS IN RELIGION AND THEOLOGY																		
284	120		Clergy Members		X					12	25	X									X
216	13	1	OCCUPATIONS IN WRITING																		
585	131		Speech Writers																	X	X
454	132		Editorial Writers																	X	X
308	137		Interpreters	X				X		9	24		X							X	

SER	DOT	NR	OCCUPATION TITLE	O	W	H	F	M	REQD	1ST	MID	O	S	A	F	N	O	A	V	2	4	G
286	139		Copywriters	X	X	X				8	28	X										X
83	139		Editors, Writers & Reporters		X	X			167	12	50	X	X								X	X
197	139		Teletext Computer Splsts—Compsn, Format, Editg						65	16	40			X	X						X	X
217	14	1	OCCUPATIONS IN ART																			
448	141		Graphic Illustrators																			
305	141		Illustrators/Commercial Artists	X						9	18			X						X		
457	141		Medical Illustrators																	X	X	X
455	142		Fashion Designers																	X	X	X
306	142		Industrial Designers	X						10	21	X									X	X
307	142		Interior Designers	X			X			8	22	X							X	X		
449	142		Layout Designers																	X		
458	142		Museum Display Artists																	X		
188	143		Photographers	X	X				91	14	21	X				X			X		X	X
444	144		Pottery Workers														X			X		X	X
452	149		Art Critics																			
181	149		Floral Designers				X		56	9	19	X				X			X		X	X
456	149		Historic Restorers																	X	X	X
459	149		Producers																	X	X	X
451	149		Taxidermists																X	X		
218	15	1	OCCUPATIONS IN ENTERTAINMENT & RECREATION																			
162	150		Actors & Actresses	X			X		26													X
441	150		Comedians	X			X												X			
163	151		Dancers	X			X		30												X	X
161	152		Musicians	X	X				138	14	28										X	X
442	152		Musicians	X	X														X			

SER	DOT	NR	OCCUPATION TITLE	O	W	H	F	M	REQD	1ST	MID	O	S	A	F	N	O	A	V	2	4	G
445	152		Singers	X								X							X			
266	153		Athletic Coaches	X						15	25		X								X	
591	153		Golf Professionals																	X		
588	153		Jockeys																X			
167	153		Professional Athletes	X					5	20	75										X	
594	153		Tennis Professionals																	X		
595	153		Umpires					X												X		
339	159		Park Rangers	X				X		11	22	X									X	
589	159		Recreation Aides																X			
34	159		Recreation Workers	X				X	135	12	17			X							X	
590	159		Scorekeepers																X			
450	159		Stage Set Designers																	X		
593	159		Stunt Performers																	X		
219	16	1	OCCUPATIONS IN ADMINISTRATIVE SPECIALIZATIONS																			
18	160		Accountants	X	X				1047	17	25				X					X		
579	160		Bank Auditors	X																	X	X
416	161		Auto. Office Work Station Analysts	X					240	18	25		X	X							X	
69	162		Buyers (Wholesale & Retail)	X	X				190	17	31		X	X		X	X			X	X	
70	162		Purchasing Agents & Buyers (not Whlsl/Retail)	X	X				244	16	31		X	X		X	X			X	X	
71	163		Sales Managers	X	X				705	12	45		X			X	X	X	X	X	X	
190	163		Telemarketing Sales Program Supervisors						65	25	100					X	X			X	X	
208	163		Teletext Senior Editors & Directors						25	30	50										X	

SER	DOT	NR	OCCUPATION TITLE	O	W	H	F	M	REQD	1ST	MID	O	S	A	F	N	O	A	V	2	4	G
16	165		Public Relations Managers	X	X				131	12	32	X									X	
20	166		Personnel & Labor Relations Workers	X	X				93	15	29		X								X	X
17	166		Personnel Administrators	X	X				405	28	50			X						X		
82	168		Estimators & Investigators	X	X				534	11	17				X		X		X	X	X	
97	168		Holographic Inspectors					X	200	18	20					X				X		
104	168		Manufacturing Inspectors					X	336	12	22		X				X	X	X	X		
258	169		Administrative Assistants	X				X		12	28						X	X	X	X		
417	169		Auto. Office Quality/Production Analysts	X					100	14	22										X	
392	169		CAD Terminal Parts Cataloguers		X				125	11	18							X				
387	169		CAG Operations Supervisors		X				20	15	25							X				
55	169		Health Service Administrators	X					220	19	50		X								X	
220	18	1	MANAGERS & OFFICIALS, n.e.c.	X																		
489	180		Nursery Managers		X				1300	16	19			X								
119	183		Blue Collar Worker Supervisors	X	X				90	15	25				X		X	X			X	
404	183		CAM Production Superintendents	X	X												X	X				
515	183		Plant Managers	X												X					X	X
21	186		Bank Officers & Administrators	X	X				643	16	29				X			X			X	X
264	187		Apartment House Managers	X	X					6	8		X				X	X				
573	187		Apartment House Managers			X																
299	187		Funeral Directors	X	X					12	28	X										
304	187		Hotel Sales Managers	X						12	20		X					X			X	
303	187		Hotel/Motel Managers	X	X					13	25		X					X			X	
352	187		Restaurant Managers			X				14	35		X									
168	188		City Managers	X					4	33	49			X				X			X	X
505	188		Police Chiefs																	X	X	X

SER	DOT	NR	OCCUPATION TITLE	O	W	H	F	M	REQD	1ST	MID	O	S	A	F	N	O	A	V	2	4	G
415	189		Auto. Office Info Management Directors	X					150	22	50											X
414	189		Auto. Office Rcds, Data, Info Security Managers	X					260	18	25											X	
412	189		Auto. Office Terminal/Msg Ctr Mgrs (Corp. Ofc)	X					500	18	37											X	
411	189		Auto. Office Terminal/Msg Ctr Mgrs (Single Ofc)	X					300	16	21											X	
333	189		Office Managers	X						11	16		X									X	
535	189		Office Supervisors																	X		
514	189		Safety Inspectors																	X		
221	19	1	MISC. PROF./TECHNICAL/ MANAGERIAL OCCUPATIONS																			
349	191		Real Estate Appraisers	X				X		13	18						X					
533	193		Airline-Radio Operators			X													X			
351	194		Recording Engineers				X			7	14								X			
177	195		Child Welfare Workers (Not household)				X	X	432	15	21		X								X	
571	195		Counselors	X																	X	X
340	195		Parole Officers	X			X			9	16										X	
31	195		Social & Recreational Workers				X		480	10	26					X					X	
566	195		Social Case Aides																	X		
570	195		Social Case Workers																		X	X
562	195		Social Directors																		X	X
165	196		Commercial Airline Pilots					X	82	31	67		X								X	
508	197		Ferryboat Operators																X			
278	197		Fishing Vessel Captains					X		12	21		X						X		X	

173

SER	DOT	NR	OCCUPATION TITLE	O	W	H	F	M	REQD	1ST	MID	O	S	A	F	N	O	A	V	2	4	G
164	199		Air Traffic Controllers	X					29	15	31		X									X
574	199		Assessors	X															X	X	X	
424	199		Business Occupations—Forecasters	X					75	17	30										X	X
395	199		CAD Engineering Software Specialists	X					360	19	30								X			
391	199		CAD Product or Systems Inspectors	X					280	12	22											
396	199		CAD Voc'l Trng & Ed Simulation Software Splsts	X					150	14	19							X	X			
403	199		CAM Holographic Inspectors	X					135	12	21											
406	199		CAM Mfg Matl/Finished Parts Traffic Controllers	X					20	12	14								X			X
405	199		CAM-CAD Software Coordinators	X					80	17	25								X			
425	199		Commerce Occupations Forecasters	X					60	16	29								X			X
383	199		Computer Modeling & Simulation Technicians	X					300	25	40								X			
90	199		Computer Programmers	X	X				258	19	27				X				X			X
421	199		Computer Software Writers—General	X	X				1830	20	30				X				X	X	X	X
89	199		Computer Systems Analysts	X		X			260	20	26				X				X	X		X
561	199		Convention Planners																X			
575	199		Credit Officers										X									
295	199		Divers					X														
426	199		Economic Occupations Forecasters	X					45	14	19								X			X

SER	DOT	NR	OCCUPATION TITLE	O	W	H	F	M	REQD	1ST	MID	O	S	A	F	N	O	A	V	2	4	G
428	199		Educational Institutions Occupations F'casters	X					20	12	20											X
470	199		Environmental Analysts																	X	X	X
538	199		Financial Aid Counselors																	X	X	X
549	199		Fund Raisers																	X	X	X
576	199		Funeral Directors																	X		
423	199		Industrial Occupations Forecasters	X					80	17	25										X	
431	199		Industrial Relations Occupations Forecasters	X					50	14	25										X	
193	199		Industrial Robot Production Technicians						800	15	24									X		
88	199		Key Punch Operators	X					200	15	21		X					X	X			
462	199		Laboratory Assistants	X														X	X			
318	199		Market Research Analysts							15	28				X							
582	199		Media Specialists																		X	
430	199		Military Occupations Forecasters	X					15	12	20										X	
583	199		Museum Curators																			
584	199		Public Relations Specialists																	X		
348	199		Quality Control Inspectors	X						7	16				X							
196	199		Robot Installation & Operations Technicians						250	12	22				X				X			
408	199		Robot On-the-Job Programmers	X					200	12	20									X		
198	199		Robot Repairmen						140	14	22								X			
356	199		Sanitary Inspectors	X				X		8	16				X							
469	199		Science Laboratory Technicians																	X		
536	199		Survey Workers																	X		

SER	DOT	NR	OCCUPATION TITLE	O	W	H	F	M	REQD	1ST	MID	O	S	A	F	N	O	A	V	2	4	G
194	199		Telemarketing Computer Programmers						60	20	35								X			
203	199		Teletext Operations Supervisors						25	20	34					X	X		X			X
202	199		Teletext Specialists—Software Programming			X			30	18	30					X	X		X			X
24	199		Urban & Regional Planners	X					31	19	35			X								X
427	199		Urban Planners Occupations Forecasters		X				20	14	21											X
429	199		Vocational Counseling/Trng Occupatns F'casters	X					20	12	20											X
222	20	1	STENOGRAPHY/TYPING/FILING OCCUPATIONS	X																		
313	201		Legal Secretaries	X						8	18		X					X	X			
321	201		Medical Secretaries	X						7	18		X					X	X			
37	203		Typists	X		X			1023	8	12		X					X	X			
372	203		Word Processing Operators	X						7	13		X					X	X			
46	206		File Clerks	X					324	8	14	X										
394	209		CAD Information Retrieval & Reproduction Clerks	X					300	10	12						X					
287	209		Court Reporters	X						12	19		X						X			
413	209		Office Info Center Terminal Operators	X					600	14	23								X	X		
36	209		Secretaries & Stenographers	X		X			3940	9	12		X					X	X	X		
367	209		Transcribing Machine Operators	X						8	12		X						X	X		
223	21	1	COMPUTING & ACCOUNT-RECORDING OCCUPATIONS	X																		
23	210		Bookkeepers	X		X			1904	10	17		X	X				X	X	X		
275	210		Bookkeeping Machine Operators	X						8	14		X	X				X	X	X		
22	211		Bank Tellers	X					531	8	12		X	X								X

SER	DOT	NR	OCCUPATION TITLE	O	W	H	F	M	REQD	1ST	MID	O	S	A	F	N	O	A	V	2	4	G
45	211		Cashiers	X					1554	12	17	X	X			X	X					
419	213		Auto. Office Data Mgmt Analysts & Supervisors	X					250	16	25										X	X
532	216		Accounting Clerks																			
42	216		Statistical Clerks	X	X				387	7	12			X					X	X		
93	219		Computer Console & Equipment Operators	X	X				558	10	18				X				X	X		
63	219		Medical Records Technicians		X				20	12	23					X	X		X	X		
204	219		Teletext Supervsrs—Library, Research, Copy, Dist						20	20	30					X	X		X	X		
224	22	1	PRODUCTION & STOCK CLERK OCCUPATIONS																		
41	222		Shipping & Receiving Clerks		X				505	8	18	X	X									
43	222		Stock Clerks & Storekeepers	X					533	8	18	X	X									
407	229		CAM Rcds Supervisors—Invntory, Stocking, Shipping		X				14	12	14								X			
225	23	1	INFORMATION & MESSAGE DISTRIBUTION OCCUPATIONS																		
40	230		Mail Carriers					X	250	19	21	X	X	X		X	X					
38	230		Postal Clerks		X				285	18	21	X	X	X		X	X					
39	235		Telephone Operators		X				316	8	10	X	X	X		X	X					
35	237		Receptionists	X					635	8	12				X		X		X			
44	238		Counter Clerks	X					350	8	15	X					O		X			
205	239		Computer Terminal Distributive Info Processors						140	20	35							X		X		
200	239		Computer Terminal Information Processors						270	20	30									X		

SER	DOT	NR	OCCUPATION TITLE	O	W	H	F	M	REQD	1ST	MID	O	S	A	F	N	O	A	V	2	4	G
507	239		Dispatchers	X																		
420	239		Electronic Mail Operations Specialists						300	12	16								X			
495	239		Security Dispatchers														X					
530	239		Telegraph Clerks														X					
342	24	1	MISCELLANEOUS CLERICAL OCCUPATIONS																			
288	241		Credit Investigators	X						7	12		X	X								
320	245		Medical Office Assistants	X						7	14		X	X				X				
371	245		Ward Clerks, Hospital			X				6	12		X	X				X				
302	249		Hotel/Motel Clerks			X		X		6	12		X	X				X				
580	249		Law Clerks																		X	X
529	249		Office Clerks															X				
539	249		Registrars																		X	X
226	25	1	SALES OCCUPATIONS & SERVICES																			
73	250		Insurance Agents, Brokers & Underwriters	X					532	14	40		X			X				X		
74	250		Real Estate Agents & Brokers	X	X				582	13	29			X		X			X	X		
534	251		Brokerage Clerks											X		X				X		
75	251		Sales Agents—Stocks & Bonds	X					67	11	50			X		X				X		
531	251		Tellers	X	X												X					
78	254		Advertising Workers						100	10	40		X		X	X				X	X	
189	254		Telemarketing Advertising & Scenario Writers						110	18	35				X	X	X			X	X	
192	254		Telemarketing Splsts—Recdg/Cust Order Take-off						80	15	30				X	X	X			X	X	

SER	DOT	NR	OCCUPATION TITLE	O	W	H	F	M	REQD	1ST	MID	O	S	A	F	N	O	A	V	2	4	G
201	254		Teletext Specialists—Marketing			X			30	18	40					X	X	X	X		X	X
199	254		Teletext Splsts—CATV Liaison & Scheduling						30	17	38					X	X	X				
386	259		CAG Sales Representatives			X		X	30	15	30							X				
552	259		Sales Representatives For Psychological Tests																X	X		
81	259		Sales Workers—Services & Construction		X	X			222	7	17			X			X					
207	259		Teletext Interactive Correspondent						30	18	25					X	X	X			X	
227	26	1	SALES OCCUPATIONS, CONSUMABLE COMMODITIES																			
435	260		Brain Food Store Operators		X																	
528	260		Food Clerks											X								
434	261		Erotic Boutique Owners		X																	
548	269		Buyers																	X	X	
544	269		Buyers Assistants											X						X	X	X
77	269		Sales Representatives—Wholesale		X	X			1001	18	33			X		X					X	
79	269		Sales Workers—Retail		X	X	X		3300	7	14			X		X						
547	269		Tobacco Buyers																X			
228	27	1	SALES OCCUPATIONS, COMMODITIES, n.e.c.		X	X	X							X								
551	271		Sales Reps For Copying Machines/Computers																		X	X
270	273		Auto Parts Salespersons		X					6	10			X				X			X	
550	273		Sales Representatives For Aircraft Equipment											X							X	X

SER	DOT	NR	OCCUPATION TITLE	O	W	H	F	M	REQD	1ST	MID	O	S	A	F	N	O	A	V	2	4	G
446	279		Antique Dealers	X					95	12	20									X		
398	279		CAD Trng & Ed Materials Salespeople	X	X														X	X		
76	279		Sales Representatives—Manufacturing	X	X				440	16	37				X						X	
229	29	1	MISCELLANEOUS SALES OCCUPATIONS																			
542	290		Department Store Sales Clerks	X	X				2345	6	14							X				
80	290		Sales Clerks—Retail	X	X			X		6	10	X	X	X								
267	294		Auctioneers	X	X					6	10	X	X	X								
545	294		Auctioneers																X			
285	299		Collection Clerks	X						7	13	X		X								
546	299		Leasing Agents																X			
325	299		Models	X						12	14			X				X				
72	299		Salespersons & Peddlers	X	X				178	8	12	X	X	X						X		
195	299		Telemarketing Sales—Shipg/Billg Clerks/Supers						50	8	18	X	X			X	X	X				
230	30	1	DOMESTIC SERVICE OCCUPATIONS																			
179	301		Housecleaners & Servants			X			491	7	14	X	X			X	X	X				
178	309		Child Care Workers (Household)			X			431	8	10	X	X			X	X	X				
231	31	1	FOOD/BEVERAGE PREPARATION & SERVICE OCCUPATIONS																			
281	310		Caterers					X	56	11	21	X	X			X	X		X			
166	310		Commercial Airline Flight Attendants					X		6	10	X	X			X	X	X	X			

SER	DOT	NR	OCCUPATION TITLE	O	W	H	F	M	REQD	1ST	MID	O	S	A	F	N	O	A	V	2	4	G
159	310		Food Counter Workers	X	X				426	7	14				X	X		X	X			
160	311		Waiters & Waitresses	X	X				1700	7	12				X	X		X	X			
157	312		Bartenders	X	X				382	10	31		X	X			X		X			
158	315		Bakers	X	X				133	9	17		X	X	X	X		X	X			
154	316		Meat Cutters & Butchers (Not plant)				X		190	12	24		X	X	X	X		X				
294	318		Dishwashers	X	X					6	7		X	X	X	X						
156	319		Food Service Workers (Commercial cooks)	X	X				4436	7	20		X	X	X	X						
553	324		Bellhops															X				
232	33	1	BARBERING/COSMETOLOGY & RELATED SVC OCCUPATIONS																	X		
557	330		Barbers																			
558	332		Beauticians																	X		
176	332		Hairdressers & Cosmetologists	X	X				565	7	14		X	X		X		X				
319	334		Masseurs/Masseuses	X						23	27		X	X			X		X			
560	338		Funeral Attendants																X			
350	34	1	AMUSEMENT & RECREATION SERVICE OCCUPATIONS																	X		
554	341		Caddies															X	X			
540	342		Amusement Park Vendors															X	X			
541	342		Cigarette Vendors															X	X			
491	349		Bouncers															X	X			
494	349		Lifeguards															X	X			
315	349		Marina Workers	X						8	13	X										

SER	DOT	NR	OCCUPATION TITLE	O	W	H	F	M	REQD	1ST	MID	O	S	A	F	N	O	A	V	2	4	G
355	35	1	MISCELLANEOUS PERSONAL SERVICE OCCUPATIONS																			
559	352		Flight Attendants																	X		
555	353		Pages/Ushers											X								
556	353		Plant Guides											X								
564	355		Hospital Orderlies											X								
463	355		Orderlies											X								
296	359		Dog Groomers	X						7	14									X		
537	359		Travel Guides																	X		
543	359		Wedding Consultants											X								
233	36	1	APPAREL & FURNISHINGS SERVICE OCCUPATIONS																			
148	369		Laundry Operators & Dry Cleaners	X					203	10	13		X			X						
501	372		Air Marshalls																		X	X
492	372		Guards											X								
493	372		Jailers											X								
173	372		Security Guards	X	X				548	12	18		X	X							X	
578	372		Store Detectives					X	14	20			X	X								
172	373		Firefighters										X									
503	375		FBI Special Agents											X							X	X
504	375		Narcotics Agents											X							X	X
499	375		Police Inspectors														X					
500	375		Police Officers														X			X		
174	375		Policemen & Detectives	X					512	15	28		X	X		X					X	
175	379		Correctional Institution Officers	X					103	12	25		X	X		X				X		

SER	DOT	NR	OCCUPATION TITLE	O	W	H	F	M	REQD	1ST	MID	O	S	A	F	N	O	A	V	2	4	G
502	379		Customs Officers																		X	X
497	379		Fire Inspectors																	X		
496	379		Fire Wardens																	X	X	
498	379		Fish and Game Wardens																	X	X	
390	38	1	BUILDING & RELATED SERVICE OCCUPATIONS																			
309	382		Janitors/Custodians	X						7	13			X					X			
467	383		Insect Pest Controllers					X											X		X	
341	383		Pest Control Workers					X		7	12			X					X		X	
234	40	1	PLANT FARMING OCCUPATIONS																			
433	405		Truffle Farmers	X			X															
183	406		Gardeners & Groundskeepers (Non-farm)	X				X	601	6	21		X			X					X	
186	409		Farm Laborers (Wage Workers)				X		895	7			X			X			X			
477	409		Farm Workers										X			X			X			
185	409		Farm Workers & Supervisors	X			X		1218	13	22		X			X			X			
184	409		Farmers & Farm Managers	X			X		1485	10	26		X									
301	409		Horticulturists	X			X						X									
490	409		Plant Propagators																		X	X
410	41	1	ANIMAL FARMING OCCUPATIONS																			
484	411		Poultry Breeders																	X		
487	412		Gamekeepers																		X	X
261	418		Animal Keepers	X			X			6	10		X							X		
476	418		Dog Groomers															X				
478	418		Horse Exercisers															X				
479	418		Horseshoers (Blacksmiths)															X				

SER	DOT	NR	OCCUPATION TITLE	O	W	H	F	M	REQD	1ST	MID	O	S	A	F	N	O	A	V	2	4	G
460	419		Animal Breeders																X	X		
475	419		Animal Keepers																X	X		
422	45	1	FORESTRY OCCUPATIONS																			
485	451		Tree Surgeons					X				X										
298	452		Foresters	X	X					13	20									X	X	
486	452		Foresters																		X	X
480	454		Loggers																		X	X
525	454		Sawmill Supervisors											X					X	X		
481	454		Tree Cutters																X	X		
482	459		Foresters Aides											X					X	X		
235	52	1	OCCUPATIONS IN PRO- CESSING FOOD/ TOBACCO PRODUCTS																			
153	525		Stock Handlers	X					941	8	12	X				X						
152	529		Food Technologists	X					15	18	30		X	X								
155	529		Packers & Wrappers (Not meat or produce)	X					600	9	14	X				X						
521	559		Chemical Operators											X						X		
526	559		Supervisors of Chemical Production											X						X	X	X
236	59	1	PROCESSING OCCU- PATIONS, n.e.c.																			
108	599		Boiler Tenders	X					62	11	24	X					X					
237	60	1	METAL MACHINING OCCUPATIONS																			
98	601		Tool & Die Makers	X					178	21	37	X					X		X	X		
518	606		Drill Press Operators															X	X			

SER	DOT	NR	OCCUPATION TITLE	O	W	H	F	M	REQD	1ST	MID	O	S	A	F	N	O	A	V	2	4	G
516	609		Bit Sharpeners		X															X		
103	609		Machine Operators		X				736	11	33		X			X	X		X			
96	609		Machinists & Job Set-up Workers		X				658	20	35			X		X	X		X			
238	61	1	METALWORKING OCCUPATIONS, n.e.c.																			
102	619		Punch Press & Stamping Operators		X				183	20	31		X			X						
99	619		Sheet Metal Workers		X				161	18	28		X					X				
239	62	1	MECHANICS & MACHINERY REPAIRERS																			
117	620		Automotive Mechanics		X				1197	9	14			X					X			
326	620		Motorcycle Repairers		X					10	16			X	X				X			
126	620		Service Station Mechanics & Attendants		X				33	8	12			X	X	X	X	X	X			
120	621		Aircraft Mechanics		X				121	15	24			X		X	X	X	X			
273	623		Boatbuilders		X			X		10	18	X	X					X				
336	623		Outboard Motor Mechanics		X			X		7	16		X	X					X			
291	631		Diesel Mechanics		X					10	23			X	X				X			
118	638		Battery Technicians—Fuel Cells		X				25	9	14				X	X	X	X	X			
523	639		Diesel Engine Testers		X			X				X								X		
109	639		Heavy Equipment Mechanics		X				963	12	17		X			X	X		X	X		
110	639		Industrial Machine Repairers		X				507	16	27		X			X	X		X			
240	65	1	PRINTING OCCUPATIONS																			
86	650		Compositors & Typesetters		X				128	18	22	X				X			X			
87	651		Printing Press Operators		X				178	17	23	X				X			X			
84	659		Lithographic Press Operators		X				81	14	17	X				X			X			

SER	DOT	NR	OCCUPATION TITLE	O	W	H	F	M	REQD	1ST	MID	O	S	A	F	N	O	A	V	2	4	G
436	66	1	WOOD MACHINING OCCUPATIONS																			
277	660		Cabinetmakers			X				10	21		X						X			
241	68	1	TEXTILE OCCUPATIONS																			
520	683		Carpet Weavers			X															X	X
522	689		Cloth Graders			X															X	X
151	689		Textile Machine Operators			X			323	9	17		X					X	X			
437	69	1	MACHINE TRADES OCCUPATIONS, n.e.c.																			
101	693		Patternmakers			X			4	18	29		X						X			
389	699		CAD Product Design Technicians			X			190	15	28								X	X		
400	699		CAM Machine & Mfg Materials Setup Mechanics			X			300	12	20								X			
402	699		CAM Production Schedulers/ Progress Controllers			X			90	12	18								X			
519	699		New Car Inspectors			X													X			
409	699		Robots—Programmed Tool Handlers			X			100	12	18											
242	70	1	OCCUPATIONS IN METAL MFR/ASSY/REPAIR, n.e.c.																			
310	700		Jewelers			X				14	20		X			X						
100	709		Assemblers			X			1670	8	20		X			X						
314	709		Locksmiths			X		X		6	18			X		X						
461	716		Instrument Repairers			X		X									X					

SER	DOT	NR	OCCUPATION TITLE	O	W	H	F	M	REQD	1ST	MID	O	S	A	F	N	O	A	V	2	4	G
243	72	1	OCCUPATIONS IN ELECTRICAL EQUIPMT ASSY/REPAIR																			
122	720		Radio & TV Mechanics	X	X				120	11	19		X				X	X	X			
124	722		A/C, Heating & Refrigeration Mechanics	X			X		207	13	19						X	X	X			
127	723		Appliance Repairers	X				X	77	10	25		X		X			X				
91	726		Computer Service Technicians			X		X	93	18	28				X	X	X	X	X			
94	729		Microcomputer Diagnosticians	X	X				200	20	35				X	X	X	X	X			
332	729		Office Machine Servicers	X	X			X		8	15		X		X			X				
527	729		Supervisors of Electronic—Computer Assembly																	X	X	
438	73	1	OCCUPATIONS IN MFR & REPAIR ASSTD MATLS PRODS																			
125	733		Office Machine Repairers	X				X	55	10	14		X				X		X			
244	74	1	PAINTING/DECORATING & RELATED OCCUPATIONS																			
141	749		Painters—Automotive	X				X	41	18	28		X				X					
142	749		Painters—Manufactured Goods	X				X	181	13	26		X				X					
245	78	1	OCCUPATIONS IN TEXTILE/LEATHER MFR & REPAIR																			
368	780		Upholsterers	X						12	17		X				X		X			
149	785		Dressmakers & Seamstresses (Non-factory)		X				107	10	24		X				X					
363	785		Tailors	X				X		6	14		X				X		X			
150	789		Sewers & Stitchers	X				X	788	9	16		X				X					

SER	DOT	NR	OCCUPATION TITLE	O	W	H	F	M	REQD	1ST	MID	O	S	A	F	N	O	A	V	2	4	G
439	80	1	OCCUPATIONS IN METAL FABRICATING, n.e.c.																			
509	801		Pipe Fitters																			
274	805		Boilermakers	X						14	22		X								X		
269	807		Auto Body Repairers	X				X		8	15				X				X			
360	809		Structural Steel Workers	X				X		15	19			X								
246	81	1	WELDING/CUTTING & RELATED OCCUPATIONS									X										
106	819		Industrial Laser Process Technicians	X				X	600	30	50			X		X						
105	819		Welders & Cutters	X				X	692	22	28			X								
247	82	1	ELECTRICAL ASSY/INSTALLING/REPAIR OCCUPATIONS									X										
113	821		Electric Power Line & Cable Maint. Mechanics	X				X	120	12	18		X			X			X			
115	822		Cable TV Installers					X	300	11	13		X			X			X			
128	822		Office Communications Equipment Installers					X	25	13	29	X				X		X	X			
114	822		Telephone Installers & Repairers					X	309	10	12		X			X			X			
132	824		Electricians (Construction)	X				X	648	20	31		X	X		X		X	X			
130	828		Electrical/Electronic Engineering Technicians	X	X				359	12	24		X	X		X		X	X			
131	828		Engineering & Science Technicians	X				X	885	10	22		X			X			X			
123	828		Home Electronic Interactive Systems Technicians			X		X	200	15	21				X	X						

SER	DOT	NR	OCCUPATION TITLE	O	W	H	F	M	REQD	1ST	MID	O	S	A	F	N	O	A	V	2	4	G
418	828		Home/Office Interactive Work System Technicians	X	X				180	14	20								X			
466	829		Electricians																		X	
191	829		Telemarketing Audio-Visual Technicians						50	25	40					X	X		X		X	
248	84	1	PAINTING/PLASTERING/WATERPROOFING/CEMENTING OCCUPATIONS																			
140	840		Painters—Construction & Maintenance	X				X	469	16	24				X	X						
147	842		Plasterers					X	24	19	28				X	X		X				
353	843		Roofers					X		8	17			X	X	X		X				
146	849		Drywall Installers & Finishers					X	84	18	28				X	X		X				
139	849		Painters & Paperhangers					X	463	15	29					X	X					
249	85	1	EXCAVATING/GRADING/PAVING OCCUPATIONS																			
144	850		Excavating, Grading & Road Machine Operators					X	456	20	30			X		X			X			
250	86	1	CONSTRUCTION OCCUPATIONS, n.e.c.																			
137	860		Carpenters					X	1185	16	28				X	X	X		X			
138	861		Bricklayers & Stonemasons					X	168	16	31				X	X			X			
143	862		Plumbers & Pipefitters			X		X	478	15	30			X		X	X		X			
300	865		Glaziers					X		8	12		X			X			X			
282	869		Cement Masons			X		X		10	22		X	X		X			X			
145	869		Construction Laborers & Carpenter Helpers					X	851	13	24				X	X	X		X			
506	869		Construction Workers																X			

SER	DOT	NR	OCCUPATION TITLE	O	W	H	F	M	REQD	1ST	MID	O	S	A	F	N	O	A	V	2	4	G
135	869		Housing Rehabilitation Technicians	X	X				1750	14	24					X	X	X				X
107	869		Operating Engineers (Construction Machinery)	X					190	21	28		X					X				X
440	89	1	STRUCTURAL WORK OCCUPATIONS, n.e.c.																			
324	899		Millwrights					X		10	20	X						X				
251	90	1	MOTOR FREIGHT OCCUPATIONS																			
95	909		Materials Utilization Technicians	X					400	15	24				X							X
171	909		Truck Drivers					X	2275	17	27		X		X	X	X	X	X			
252	91	1	TRANSPORTATION OCCUPATIONS, n.e.c.																			
354	911		Sailors					X		15	22	X										
170	913		Bus Drivers					X	127	10	22		X			X	X	X	X			
187	919		Travel Agents						52	10	18			X								
253	92	1	PACKAGING & MATERIALS HANDLING OCCUPATIONS	X										X								X
112	921		Crane, Derrick & Hoist Operators	X					148	12	17		X			X	X	X				
111	922		Fork Lift & Tow Motor Operators	X					366	8	13		X					X				
182	922		Freight & Materials Handlers	X					722	10	24	X						X	X			
254	95	1	UTILITIES PRODUCTION & DISTRIBUTION OCCUPATIONS									X										
134	952		Energy Conservation Technicians	X				X	1500	13	26				X			X				

SER	DOT	NR	OCCUPATION TITLE	O	W	H	F	M	REQD	1ST	MID	O	S	A	F	N	O	A	V	2	4	G
136	955		Hazardous Waste Disposal Technicians	X				X	1500	15	28					X			X	X	X	X
133	955		Waste & Water Treatment Plant Operators	X						41	12	14		X		X			X			X
116	959		Energy Auditors					X	150	12	16				X	X		X			X
255	96	1	AMUSEMENT/RECREATION/TV OCCUPATIONS, n.e.c.																		
443	962		Artistic Program Assistants	X									X					X			
263	969		Announcers (Radio & TV)	X						11	35		X					X	X	X	X
121	969		Broadcast Technicians	X					17	12	14		X	X				X	X	X
293	969		Disc Jockeys	X						9	28		X	X				X	X	X
256	97	1	OCCUPATIONS IN GRAPHIC ART WORK																		
337	970		Painters, Sign	X				X		7	15		X					X		
343	971		Photoengravers	X						10	12	X						X		
85	972		Lithographers	X					45	27	38		X				X	X	X
289	976		Darkroom Laboratory Technicians	X						7	15	X	X					X	
524	976		Film Processing Supervisors																		
464	976		Photographic Laboratory Workers	X												X			X	
344	976		Photographic Process Workers	X						7	12	X						X	
517	979		Book Trimmers																		
384	979		CAG Layout Artists	X					40	10	18					X		X	X
385	979		CAG Terminal Input Artists	X					40	17	18					X		X	X
381	979		Computer Graphics Technician	X					150	20	35					X		X	X
129	979		Engineering Draftsmen		X				335	10	22	X				X	X	X	X

191

SAMPLE COVER LETTER 1

1. August 5, 1983

2. Mr. George Giorgi, Supervisor
   Field Service Department
   Wow Company
   1118 Main Street
   Wichita, KS 66002

3. Dear Mr. Giorgi

4. As you may recall, I spoke with you on the telephone on Thursday, August 4, regarding my interest in working for your organization as a field service representative.

5. In two weeks, I will complete my training curriculum which consists of over 700 hours of training and hands-on experience with central processors and all major peripheral devices. I have excellent communication skills, interact well with people, and am willing to travel and relocate.

6. Enclosed is a copy of my resume which provides details about my background. I will telephone you on Monday, August 8, to set up an interview.

7. Sincerely,

8. Sally Smith
   P.O. Box O
   Reading, PA
   (800) 600-7000

SAMPLE COVER LETTER 2

1. May 5, 1984

2. W. A. Benson, Director
   Personnel Department
   Benson Communications
   Wichita, KS 66002

3. Dear Mr. Benson:

4. Your company was recommended to me by your former employee, Mr. Andrew Baker. I have worked in the fields of computers, communications, and sales for ten years and would like to combine this experience as a marketing representative for your company.

5. My education has been strong in the areas of computer science and electronics, and I have operated a large-scale system. I have had sales experience on a commission basis. My years as a teacher have enhanced my communication skills.

   Enclosed is a copy of my resume which details my experience in education, sales, electronics, and computer science.

6. I will phone you on Wednesday morning, May 13, to set up a time for an interview.

7. Sincerely,

8. P. G. Terry
   4004 Warwick Boulevard
   Apartment 314
   Wichita, KS 66001
   (316) 655-4937

SAMPLE RESUME 1
(Combination)
John Jones
6219 Blaisdell Street
See, California 92376
(800) 671-3098

OBJECTIVE

To obtain a computer programmer position with a progressive, growing firm. Have solid background in four computer languages. Am self-reliant, disciplined, and enjoy a challenging environment.

EDUCATION

1/81–3/82

Control Data Institute, Anaheim, California

Demonstrated ability to work independently by successfully completing self-paced, individualized program in Computer Programming and Operations. Accurately wrote, debugged, and documented programs in COBOL, Assembly, FORTRAN and RPGII computer languages. Completed additional coursework including Data Processing Concepts and Operations, Systems Design and Accounting.

2/76–6/77

Mt. San Antonio Community College, Walnut, California

Completed a variety of general courses.

EXPERIENCE

Management

Directed planning and implementation of all aspects of theater lighting. Trained and supervised theater company personnel. Prepared designs and layouts for effective advertising of productions.

Sales

Demonstrated ability to maintain positive relations with customers. Commended for consistent accuracy in cash transactions.

Electrical/Mechanical

Solved mechanical and electrical problems on a variety of types of medical equipment. Personally responsible for all on-call service for a large hospital.

Clerical

Maintained accurate supply inventory and issue records.

CHRONOLOGY:

12/80–Present	7-Eleven, Covina, California
9/78–12/80	Powell's Hardware, Claremont, California
1/77–7/80	Actor's Repertory Theatre, Claremont, California
9/75–1/76	Tru-Etch, El Monte, California
8/72–8/75	U.S. Army
10/71–7/72	Pomona Fish Market, Pomona, California
11/68–9/71	Pomona Valley Community Hospital, Pomona, California

COMMENT

Pride self on always striving for excellence.

SAMPLE RESUME 2
(Chronological)

Sandy Jones
4852 Second Street
Muncie, Ind.

PROFESSIONAL GOAL
A position in communications involving
high-technology messages.

EDUCATION
M.S. Technological Sciences, 1981—University of California,
Irvine. Dean's Honor List, National Science Foundation
Grant.

B.A. Communications, 1979—University of Minnesota,
Minneapolis. Emphasized science reporting. Knowledge
of statistical and computer applications.

EXPERIENCE
SPACE REPORTER. Miami Herald, Miami, FL (July
1982–present). Covered all space launches during this
time frame. Monitored and reported on space program
development in Washington, D.C., in both the
legislative and executive branches. Developed a series
on the legacy of space from previous missions that
won the National Press Association award for
excellence.

SCIENCE REPORTER. Milwaukee Tribune, Milwaukee,
WI (June 1981–June 1982). Covered a variety of
science subjects, including the release of toxins into
local rivers, the effects of acid rain on the state's water
bodies, and organ transplants at the city's medical
facilities. Developed these stories, and their sources.
Won the state press association award for excellence
in reporting.

INTERN. St. Paul Dispatch. St. Paul, MN, (June
1977–June 1979). Worked as a copy aide on the
business and sports news desks. Assimilated and
explained statistical information from stock tables,
contributed to a daily business news column. Covered
several dozen high school and junior college athletic
events. Received a scholarship for the newspaper for
my senior year.

RELATED ACTIVITIES
Photography, magazine writing, hiking and downhill
skiing.

November 1984

SAMPLE THANK-YOU LETTER

1. April 21, 1984

2. Ms. Julie Cooper
   Marketing Department
   ABC Office Supply
   5759 Waterbury Circle
   Des Moines, IA 55041

3. Dear Ms. Cooper:

4. I want to thank you for talking with me about the
   position of marketing researcher this afternoon.

5. On the basis of your description of the costing experience
   required, I am certain that my background and extensive
   studies and experience in macro-economics qualify me
   for the position.

6. I am interested in ABC as a company and was impressed
   with your professionalism and methods of doing
   business. I would be proud to be a part of your
   organization.

7. Many thanks for considering me for the position. If I
   have not heard from you by the 28th of April, I would
   like to phone you to check on what progress has been
   made.

   Once again, thank you for the time you gave me this
   afternoon.

8. Sincerely,

9. Bill Jones
   111 First Avenue
   Anytown, USA
   Home phone: (800) 634-8780
   Office phone: (800) 725-9119

be7261S-DS

APPENDIX B

RANKINGS OF COLLEGES AND UNIVERSITIES

THE RATINGS GAME: WHO'S ON FIRST

Rankings, ratings, surveys and polls are only as good as the groups gathering the information. Often, a well-done survey can help in the decision-making process, whether it be for a refrigerator or an academic education.

As we searched through endless stacks of research on higher education, we came across two surveys we think you can count on.

The first, conducted by the prestigious National Academy of Sciences (NAS), rates the *research-doctorate* programs in the United States. The NAS took into account such factors as program size, publication records, university library size and what graduates were like. It covered five major academic divisions—mathematical and physical sciences, humanities, engineering, biological sciences, and social/behavioral sciences—and looked at a total of thirty-two disciplines (precise subjects) over the five academic areas.

This appendix includes the NAS overall ranking, which shows the University of California—Berkeley as number one, and the program rankings by academic division. Please study the rankings by particular discipline as well. You may discover that a school rates high in humanities, for example, but low in English as part of the humanities (bad news if you wanted to be English teacher).

The second study, Selective Guide to Colleges 1982–1983, by Edward B. Fiske, respected education editor of *The New York Times,* is more well-rounded. On page 237 it evaluates undergraduate degrees at schools by looking at three areas: academic, social and quality of life (there is more to student life than hitting the books, after all). The authors derived overall rankings by simply adding the scores in the three areas. Watch especially for those schools earning a "5" in academics, the highest score possible.

NAS REPORT
PROGRAM RANKINGS
(overall I)

UNIVERSITY	RAW SCORE	STANDARDIZED
1. University of California—Berkeley	480	84.6
2. University of California—Los Angeles	347.5	61.3
3. Stanford University	346.5	61.1
4. University of Wisconsin—Madison	344.5	60.8
5. Harvard University	333	58.7
6. University of Michigan	322.5	56.9
7. Yale University	321	56.6
8. Massachusetts Institute of Technology	308	54.3
9. Princeton University	250	44.1
10. University of Chicago	227	40.0
11. Cornell University	226.5	39.9
12. University of Pennsylvania	222	39.1
13. University of Illinois—Urbana/ Champaign	198.5	35.0
14. University of Texas—Austin	195	34.4
15. University of Minnesota	184.5	32.5
16. Columbia University	153.5	27.1
17. University of Washington	133	23.4
18. Indiana University	129	22.7
19. Purdue University	105.5	18.6
University of California—Davis	105.5	18.6
21. Duke University	103	18.2
22. University of North Carolina	99.5	17.5
23. Northwestern University	86	15.2
24. California Institute of Technology	73.5	13.0
Ohio State University	73.5	13.0
26. New York University	72	12.7
27. Rockefeller University	65.5	11.5
28. Pennsylvania State University	60.5	10.7
29. Brown University	52.5	9.3
30. University of California—San Diego	51.5	9.1
	5670.5	999.9

NAS REPORT
PROGRAM RANKINGS
(by academic division)

MATHEMATICAL & PHYSICAL SCIENCES

UNIVERSITY-PROGRAM	SCORE
1. Stanford University	9.7
2. University of California—Berkeley	9.1
3. Massachusetts Institute of Technology	8.8
4. University of Wisconsin—Madison	7.5
5. University of California—Los Angeles	6.4
6. Cornell University	6.2
7. University of Illinois—Urbana/Champaign	6.1
8. Harvard University	5.4
9. University of Chicago	5.2
10. California Institute of Technology	4.5
11. Columbia University	4.4
12. Princeton University	3.7
University of Texas—Austin	3.7
14. Purdue University	3.6
15. University of Minnesota	3.0
16. University of Maryland	2.5
17. University of Michigan	2.4
18. University of Washington	2.4
19. Yale University	2.1
20. New York University	1.6
SUNY at Stony Brook	1.6

HUMANITIES

UNIVERSITY	SCORE
1. Yale University	8.3
2. Princeton University	8.1
3. University of Michigan	7.2
4. University of California—Berkeley	7.1
5. Stanford University	6.7
6. Harvard University	6.6
7. University of California—Los Angeles	6.5
8. University of Texas—Austin	6.2
9. Cornell University	5.5
10. Indiana University	5.4
11. University of Pennsylvania	4.6
12. University of Chicago	4.3
13. University of Illinois—Urbana/Champaign	3.9
14. Columbia University	3.5
University of Wisconsin—Madison	3.5
16. New York University	2.8
17. University of North Carolina	2.7
18. University of Pittsburgh	2.5
19. University of Minnesota	2.5
20. University of Massachusetts	2.1

ENGINEERING

UNIVERSITY	SCORE
1. Massachusetts Institute of Technology	10.7
2. University of California—Berkeley	10.4
3. University of Illinois—Urbana/Champaign	9.2
4. Purdue University	8.1
5. Stanford University	7.3
6. University of Minnesota	6.3
7. Northwestern University	5.1
8. University of Michigan	5.0
9. Princeton University	4.9
10. Cornell University	4.5
11. University of California—Los Angeles	4.4
12. Pennsylvania State University	3.4
13. University of Wisconsin—Madison	3.2
14. University of Texas—Austin	2.8
Georgia Institute of Technology	2.8
16. University of Delaware	2.5
Rensselaer Polytechnic Institute	2.5
18. University of Southern California	2.3
19. Carnegie-Mellon University	2.3
20. Brown University	2.2

BIOLOGICAL SCIENCES

UNIVERSITY	SCORE
1. University of California—Davis	9.7
2. University of Wisconsin—Madison	8.7
3. University of California—Berkeley	8.3
4. Harvard University	8.3
5. University of California—Los Angeles	7.7
6. Yale University	7.3
7. University of Pennsylvania	7.0
8. Rockefeller University	6.3
9. Duke University	6.1
10. University of Washington	5.9
11. Massachusetts Institute of Technology	5.1
12. University of Michigan	3.8
13. University of California—San Diego	2.5
14. Cornell University	2.2
15. University of Georgia	2.0
16. University of Texas—Austin	2.0
17. University of Chicago	1.8
University of Illinois—Urbana/Champaign	1.8
19. Stanford University	1.7
20. Washington University—St. Louis	1.7

SOCIAL & BEHAVIORAL SCIENCES

UNIVERSITY	SCORE
1. University of California—Berkeley	9.0
2. University of Michigan	8.8
3. University of Wisconsin—Madison	7.8
4. Yale University	7.8
5. Harvard University	7.1
6. University of Chicago	7.1
7. Stanford University	5.6
8. University of California—Los Angeles	5.3
9. University of Minnesota	5.0
10. University of Pennsylvania	5.0
11. Massachusetts Institute of Technology	4.5
12. University of Illinois—Urbana/Champaign	4.3
13. Princeton University	4.0
14. Indiana University	3.7
15. Columbia University	3.0
16. University of North Carolina	2.7
17. Ohio State University	2.6
18. Duke University	2.5
19. Northwestern University	2.2
20. University of Washington	2.1

NAS REPORT
PROGRAM RANKINGS
(by discipline)

CHEMISTRY

UNIVERSITY-PROGRAM	SCORE
1. University of Wisconsin—Madison	4.5
2. California Institute of Technology	4.4
3. Massachusetts Institute of Technology	4.4
4. University of Illinois—Urbana/Champaign	4.4
5. University of California—Berkeley	4.3
6. University of California—Los Angeles	4.2
7. Cornell University	4.2
8. Harvard University	4.1
9. Purdue University	4.1
10. Columbia University	4.1
Stanford University	4.1
12. Northwestern University	3.9
13. University of Texas—Austin	3.9
14. University of Chicago	3.9
15. Ohio State University	3.9
16. Texas A & M University	3.8
17. Colorado University	3.8
Yale University	3.8
19. University of Southern California	3.8
20. Princeton University	3.7
21. University of California—San Diego	3.7
Indiana University	3.7
23. University of Minnesota	3.7
24. University of Utah	3.7
25. University of North Carolina	3.7

COMPUTER SCIENCE

UNIVERSITY-PROGRAM	SCORE
1. Stanford University	6.3
2. Massachusetts Institute of Technology	6.0
3. University of Illinois—Urbana/Champaign	5.8
4. University of California—Berkeley	5.4
5. Carnegie-Mellon University	5.4
6. Cornell University	5.3
7. University of California—Los Angeles	5.2
8. University of Wisconsin—Madison	5.0
9. University of Texas—Austin	5.0
10. University of Maryland	4.8
11. Pennsylvania State University	4.7
12. Yale University	4.7
13. University of Minnesota	4.7
14. University of Utah	4.7
15. SUNY at Stony Brook	4.6
16. University of Massachusetts	4.6
17. Syracuse University	4.5
18. University of Pennsylvania	4.5
19. Georgia Institute of Technology	4.4
20. New York University	4.4

GEOSCIENCES

UNIVERSITY-PROGRAM	SCORE
1. Massachusetts Institute of Technology	5.7
2. Columbia University	5.6
3. University of California—Los Angeles	5.4
4. California Institute of Technology	5.4
5. University of Texas—Austin	5.2
6. Harvard University	5.1
7. University of Chicago	5.1
8. University of Wisconsin—Madison	5.0
9. University of Michigan	5.0
10. University of California—Berkeley—Geology	4.9
11. Yale University	4.8
12. Princeton University—Geological & Geophysical Sciences	4.8
13. Arizona University	4.8
14. Stanford University—Geology	4.8
15. University of Washington	4.7
16. Brown University	4.7
17. SUNY at Stony Brook	4.7
18. Cornell University	4.7
Pennsylvania State University	4.7
20. Johns Hopkins University	4.6

MATHEMATICS

UNIVERSITY-PROGRAM	SCORE
1. University of California—Berkeley	5.6
2. Princeton University	5.5
3. University of Wisconsin—Madison	5.4
4. Massachusetts Institute of Technology	5.4
5. New York University	5.3
6. Stanford University	5.3
7. University of Chicago	5.1
8. University of Illinois	5.1
9. University of California—Los Angeles	5.0
10. Harvard University	5.0
11. Purdue University	4.9
12. University of Minnesota	4.9
13. Brown University	4.8
14. Rutgers University	4.8
15. Maryland University—Mathematics	4.7
16. Northwestern University	4.7
17. University of Michigan	4.7
18. Columbia University	4.6
19. University of California—San Diego	4.6
20. University of North Carolina	4.6

PHYSICS

UNIVERSITY-PROGRAM	SCORE
1. Massachusetts Institute of Technology	6.0
2. Harvard University	5.6
3. Stanford University—Physics	5.4
4. University of Illinois—Urbana/Champaign	5.3
5. Cornell University	5.2
6. Stanford University—Applied Physics	5.2
7. University of Chicago	5.2
8. University of California—Berkeley	5.1
9. California Institute of Technology	5.0
10. Princeton University	4.9
11. University of California—Los Angeles	4.8
Maryland University	4.8
13. University of Pennsylvania	4.8
14. SUNY at Stony Brook	4.7
15. University of Pittsburgh	4.7
University of Washington	4.7
17. University of Texas—Austin	4.7
18. University of Rochester	4.6
19. University of California—San Diego	4.6
20. Columbia University	4.6

STATISTICS/BIOSTATISTICS

UNIVERSITY-PROGRAM	SCORE
1. University of California—Berkeley	5.9
2. Stanford University	5.5
3. Cornell University	5.1
4. Purdue University	5.1
5. University of Wisconsin—Madison	5.1
6. University of Minnesota	5.0
7. University of Washington	5.0
8. Columbia University	4.9
9. Iowa State University	4.9
10. University of Rochester	4.7
11. University of Michigan—Statistics	4.6
12. Florida State University	4.5
Rutgers University	4.5
14. University of Chicago	4.5
15. University of North Carolina—Biostatistics	4.4
North Carolina State University—Statistics	4.4
17. University of North Carolina—Statistics	4.4
18. Ohio State University	4.3
19. Pennsylvania State University	4.3
20. Michigan State University	4.3
University of California—Los Angeles	4.3

ART HISTORY

UNIVERSITY-PROGRAM	SCORE
1. New York University	6.3
2. Yale University	6.2
3. Columbia University	5.9
4. Harvard University	5.8
5. Princeton University	5.7
6. University of Michigan	5.3
7. Stanford University	5.3
8. University of California—Berkeley	5.2
9. University of Pennsylvania	5.0
10. Johns Hopkins University	5.0
11. Indiana University	4.9
12. University of California—Los Angeles	4.7
13. University of Chicago	4.6
14. University of North Carolina	4.6
15. Bryn Mawr College	4.5
16. University of Pittsburgh	4.5
17. Northwestern University	4.3
18. University of Wisconsin—Madison	4.1
19. Boston University	4.1
20. Cornell University	3.8

CLASSICS

UNIVERSITY-PROGRAM	SCORE
1. Harvard University	6.4
2. University of California—Berkeley	6.1
3. Yale University	5.8
4. University of Michigan	5.8
5. Princeton University	5.7
6. University of North Carolina	5.6
University of Texas—Austin	5.6
8. Stanford University	5.5
9. Bryn Mawr College	5.2
10. Brown University	4.9
11. University of Minnesota	4.8
12. Duke University	4.7
13. Ohio State University	4.6
14. University of Illinois—Urbana/Champaign	4.6
15. Columbia University	4.2
16. Cornell University	4.2
17. University of Pennsylvania	4.2
18. SUNY at Buffalo	4.1
19. University of Chicago	4.0
20. University of Cincinnati	3.9

ENGLISH LANGUAGE & LITERATURE

UNIVERSITY-PROGRAM	SCORE
1. Yale University	5.3
2. University of California—Berkeley	5.3
3. Cornell University	5.3
4. Stanford University	5.3
5. Harvard University	5.2
6. University of California—Los Angeles	5.2
7. Princeton University	5.1
8. University of Michigan	5.1
9. University of Virginia	5.1
10. Indiana University	5.1
11. University of Chicago	5.0
12. University of Pennsylvania	4.9
13. University of Texas—Austin	4.9
14. University of Wisconsin—Madison	4.8
15. Columbia University	4.8
University of North Carolina	4.8
17. Johns Hopkins University	4.7
18. Michigan State University	4.7
19. SUNY at Buffalo	4.7
University of Washington	4.7

FRENCH LANGUAGE & LITERATURE

UNIVERSITY-PROGRAM	SCORE
1. Yale University	5.9
2. New York University	5.6
3. Columbia University	5.5
4. Princeton University	5.4
5. Cornell University	5.3
6. University of Illinois—Urbana/Champaign	5.2
7. Indiana University	5.2
8. University of Pennsylvania	5.0
9. Stanford University	4.9
10. University of Texas—Austin	4.9
11. University of California—Berkeley	4.9
12. University of Michigan	4.8
13. University of Virginia	4.8
14. University of Wisconsin—Madison	4.7
15. University of North Carolina	4.7
16. Pennsylvania State University	4.6
University of Washington	4.6
18. University of Kansas	4.6
19. Brown University	4.6
CUNY—Graduate School	4.6

GERMAN LANGUAGE & LITERATURE

UNIVERSITY-PROGRAM	SCORE
1. Indiana University	5.8
2. Yale University	5.6
3. Princeton University	5.4
4. Stanford University	5.3
5. University of California—Berkeley	5.3
University of California—Los Angeles	5.3
7. University of Wisconsin—Madison	5.2
8. University of Texas—Austin	5.2
9. University of Michigan	5.2
10. Cornell University	5.1
11. University of Illinois—Urbana/Champaign	5.1
12. Ohio State University	4.9
13. University of Massachusetts	4.9
University of Washington	4.9
15. University of Minnesota	4.6
16. University of Cincinnati	4.5
17. Washington University—St. Louis	4.5
18. University of North Carolina	4.4
19. Harvard University	4.4
20. University of Pennsylvania	4.3

LINGUISTICS

UNIVERSITY-PROGRAM	SCORE
1. University of California—Los Angeles	5.8
2. University of Texas—Austin	5.6
3. Massachusetts Institute of Technology	5.5
4. University of Pennsylvania	5.3
5. University of Chicago	5.3
6. University of Massachusetts	5.3
7. University of California—Berkeley	5.1
University of Illinois—Urbana/Champaign	5.1
9. University of California—San Diego	5.1
10. Harvard University	4.9
11. Stanford University	4.9
12. University of Hawaii	4.9
13. University of Connecticut	4.8
Cornell University	4.8
15. Ohio State University	4.7
16. University of Michigan	4.7
17. Yale University	4.6
18. CUNY—Graduate School	4.6
19. Indiana University	4.4
20. Georgetown University	4.4

MUSIC

UNIVERSITY-PROGRAM	SCORE
1. University of Michigan	5.9
2. University of Chicago	5.5
3. Yale University	5.4
4. Princeton University	5.2
5. University of California—Los Angeles	5.2
University of Illinois—Urbana/Champaign	5.2
7. University of Rochester	5.1
8. University of California—Berkeley	5.0
Indiana University	5.0
10. Cornell University	4.9
11. Peabody Institute of Johns Hopkins University	4.8
12. University of Iowa	4.8
13. University of Texas—Austin	4.8
14. Columbia University	4.8
University of Southern California	4.8
Stanford University	4.8
17. Northwestern University	4.7
18. CUNY—Graduate School	4.7
Ohio State University	4.7
20. University of North Carolina	4.7

PHILOSOPHY

UNIVERSITY-PROGRAM	SCORE
1. Princeton University	5.7
2. University of Pittsburgh—Philosophy	5.7
3. Harvard University	5.5
4. University of California—Berkeley	5.4
5. University of Michigan	5.2
6. University of Pittsburgh—History and philosophy of Science	5.2
7. Stanford University	5.1
8. University of California—Los Angeles	5.0
9. University of Chicago	4.9
10. Massachusetts Institute of Technology	4.9
11. University of Minnesota	4.9
12. University of Massachusetts	4.9
13. Cornell University	4.9
14. University of Wisconsin—Madison	4.8
15. Catholic University of America	4.7
16. Boston University	4.6
University of North Carolina	4.6
Ohio State University	4.6
University of Texas—Austin	4.6
20. Columbia University	4.6

SPANISH LANGUAGE & LITERATURE

UNIVERSITY-PROGRAM	SCORE
1. University of Texas—Austin	5.9
2. Harvard University	5.4
3. University of California—Berkeley	5.2
4. University of Wisconsin—Madison	5.2
5. University of Pennsylvania	5.2
6. Indiana University	5.2
7. University of California—Los Angeles	5.1
8. University of Kansas	5.1
University of Minnesota	5.1
10. Yale University	5.0
11. University of Illinois—Urbana/Champaign	5.0
12. Cornell University	4.8
13. Princeton University	4.8
14. University of Arizona	4.7
SUNY at Buffalo	4.7
16. University of Michigan	4.7
17. New York University	4.7
18. University of North Carolina	4.7
University of Puerto Rico	4.7
20. University of Massachusetts	4.6

CHEMICAL ENGINEERING

UNIVERSITY-PROGRAM	SCORE
1. University of California—Berkeley	5.9
2. Massachusetts Institute of Technology	5.7
3. University of Delaware	5.6
4. University of Minnesota	5.5
5. University of Wisconsin—Madison	5.4
6. Purdue University	5.4
7. University of Illinois—Urbana/Champaign	5.2
8. University of Houston	5.0
9. Northwestern University	4.9
10. California Institute of Technology	4.9
11. Princeton University	4.8
12. Pennsylvania State University	4.7
13. University of Massachusetts	4.7
14. University of Michigan	4.7
University of Pennsylvania	4.7
University of Texas—Austin	4.7
17. University of Rochester	4.7
18. SUNY at Buffalo	4.6
19. University of Maryland	4.6
20. Carnegie-Mellon University	4.5

CIVIL ENGINEERING

UNIVERSITY-PROGRAM	SCORE
1. University of California—Berkeley	5.6
2. Massachusetts Institute of Technology	5.5
3. University of Illinois—Urbana/Champaign	5.5
4. Stanford University	5.2
5. Cornell University	5.2
6. Colorado State University	5.0
7. Northwestern University	4.9
Purdue University	4.9
9. University of Texas—Austin	4.8
10. Georgia Institute of Technology	4.8
11. University of California—Los Angeles	4.6
University of Michigan	4.6
13. Virginia Polytechnic Institute	4.6
14. University of Wisconsin—Madison	4.5
15. University of Washington	4.5
16. Princeton University	4.4
17. University of Colorado	4.3
18. University of California—Davis	4.3
19. Iowa State University	4.2
University of Southern California	4.2
Utah State University	4.2

ELECTRICAL ENGINEERING

UNIVERSITY-PROGRAM	SCORE
1. Massachusetts Institute of Technology	6.3
2. University of Illinois—Urbana/Champaign	6.1
3. Stanford University	6.1
4. University of California—Berkeley	6.1
5. Purdue University	5.2
6. University of Southern California	5.0
7. University of California—Los Angeles	5.0
8. Carnegie-Mellon University	5.0
9. University of Minnesota	4.8
10. University of Michigan	4.8
11. Cornell University	4.7
12. Princeton University	4.7
13. Pennsylvania State University	4.6
14. University of Colorado	4.5
15. University of Maryland	4.5
Georgia Institute of Technology	4.5
17. Rensselaer Polytechnic Institute	4.5
18. Brown University	4.5
19. University of Massachusetts	4.5
University of Wisconsin—Madison	4.5

MECHANICAL ENGINEERING

UNIVERSITY-PROGRAM	SCORE
1. Massachusetts Institute of Technology	6.1
2. University of California—Berkeley	5.8
3. Stanford University	5.5
4. University of Minnesota	5.5
5. University of Illinois—Urbana/Champaign	5.2
6. Purdue University	5.2
7. Rensselaer Polytechnic Institute	5.2
8. Brown University	5.1
9. Northwestern University	5.0
10. Princeton University	4.9
11. University of Michigan	4.8
12. University of California—Los Angeles	4.7
13. Pennsylvania State University	4.7
14. Cornell University	4.7
15. University of Wisconsin—Madison	4.7
16. University of Virginia	4.6
17. Georgia Institute of Technology	4.6
18. Carnegie-Mellon University	4.6
University of Texas—Austin	4.6
20. California Institute of Technology	4.5

BIOCHEMISTRY

UNIVERSITY-PROGRAM	SCORE
1. Harvard University—Biochemistry & Molecular Biology	4.8
2. Yale University	4.7
3. Stanford University	4.7
4. Massachusetts Institute of Technology	4.6
5. Harvard University—Biological Chemistry (Medical School)	4.6
6. University of California—Berkeley	4.6
7. University of Wisconsin—Madison	4.6
8. University of California—San Francisco	4.5
9. Rockefeller University	4.4
University of California—Los Angeles	4.4
11. University of Pennsylvania	4.4
12. Cornell University—Ithaca	4.3
13. University of Washington	4.2
University of Chicago	4.2
15. University of California—Davis	4.2
16. Duke University	4.2
17. University of Michigan	4.1
University of California—San Diego—Chemistry	4.1
19. Johns Hopkins University	4.1
20. Columbia University	4.1
21. University of California—San Diego—Biology	4.1
22. Brandeis University	4.0
23. Northwestern University	4.0

BOTANY

UNIVERSITY-PROGRAM	SCORE
1. University of California—Davis—Plant Physiology	5.8
2. University of California—Davis—Botany	5.6
3. University of California—Davis—Plant Pathology	5.4
4. University of California—Berkeley—Botany	5.3
5. University of Wisconsin—Madison—Botany	5.2
6. University of Michigan	5.2
7. Cornell University	5.1
8. University of Wisconsin—Madison—Plant Pathology	5.0
9. University of California—Berkeley—Plant Physiology	5.0
10. Duke University	4.9
University of Georgia—Botany	4.9
University of Illinois—Urbana/Champaign—Botany	4.9
13. University of Texas—Austin	4.9
University of Illinois—Urbana/Champaign—Plant Pathology and Plant Physiology	4.9
15. Michigan State University	4.8
16. University of California—Los Angeles	4.7
17. University of California—Riverside	4.7
18. Yale University	4.7
19. North Carolina State University—Botany	4.6
20. University of Washington	4.6

CELLULAR/MOLECULAR BIOLOGY

UNIVERSITY-PROGRAM	SCORE
1. University of Wisconsin—Madison	5.7
2. Yale University	5.6
3. Harvard University	5.5
4. Massachusetts Institute of Technology	5.4
5. Rockefeller University	5.4
6. University of California—Berkeley	5.1
7. California Institute of Technology	5.1
University of California—Los Angeles	5.1
9. University of California—San Diego	5.0
10. University of Chicago—Genetics	4.9
11. Duke University	4.9
12. University of Pennsylvania	4.9
13. University of Colorado	4.8
Columbia University	4.8
15. University of Washington	4.8
16. Washington University—St. Louis	4.7
17. Baylor College of Medicine	4.7
18. Purdue University	4.6
19. Brandeis University	4.6
20. Johns Hopkins University	4.6

MICROBIOLOGY

UNIVERSITY-PROGRAM	SCORE
1. Rockefeller University	5.5
2. Massachusetts Institute of Technology	5.0
3. University of Pennsylvania—Immunology	5.0
4. University of California—Los Angeles	4.9
5. University of Pennsylvania—Microbiology	4.9
6. University of California—Davis	4.6
Duke University	4.6
8. University of Washington	4.6
9. University of California—San Diego	4.5
University of Wisconsin—Madison	4.5
University of Alabama—Birmingham	4.5
12. University of Michigan	4.5
13. New York University	4.5
14. Columbia University	4.3
University of Minnesota	4.3
16. Michigan State University	4.3
17. University of North Carolina	4.3
18. University of Rochester	4.2
19. Yale University	4.2
20. University of Illinois—Urbana/Champaign	4.2
21. University of Chicago—Virology	4.2
22. Rutgers University	4.2

PHYSIOLOGY

UNIVERSITY-PROGRAM	SCORE
1. University of Pennsylvania	5.8
2. University of San Francisco	5.7
3. Rockefeller University	5.7
4. University of California—Los Angeles	5.4
Yale University	5.4
6. University of Washington	5.3
7. Harvard University	5.1
8. University of Michigan	5.0
Washington University—St. Louis	5.0
10. University of Rochester	4.9
11. Duke University	4.9
12. University of California—Davis	4.9
13. University of California—Berkeley	4.8
14. University of Iowa	4.7
15. Johns Hopkins University	4.7
16. University of Wisconsin—Madison	4.6
17. Purdue University	4.6
18. University of Virginia	4.5
19. University of North Carolina	4.5
20. University of Alabama—Birmingham	4.5

ZOOLOGY

UNIVERSITY-PROGRAM	SCORE
1. University of California—Berkeley	5.9
2. University of Washington	5.9
3. Harvard University	5.7
4. Yale University	5.6
5. University of California—Los Angeles	5.5
6. University of California—Davis	5.3
7. Duke University	5.2
8. University of Texas—Austin	5.1
9. University of Wisconsin—Madison	5.1
10. University of Georgia	4.9
11. University of California—Irvine	4.8
12. University of Colorado	4.8
13. University of North Carolina	4.7
14. University of Massachusetts	4.6
15. Michigan State University	4.6
16. Ohio State University	4.5
Oregon State University	4.5
18. University of Iowa	4.5
19. University of Arizona	4.4
20. University of Minnesota	4.4

ANTHROPOLOGY

UNIVERSITY-PROGRAM	SCORE
1. University of Michigan	5.9
2. University of Chicago	5.7
3. University of California—Berkeley	5.6
4. Yale University	5.3
5. University of Arizona	5.2
6. Stanford University	5.1
7. Harvard University	5.1
University of Pennsylvania	5.1
9. University of Illinois—Urbana/Champaign	5.1
10. Northwestern University	5.0
11. Columbia University	5.0
12. Duke University	4.9
13. University of California—Los Angeles	4.9
14. CUNY—Graduate School	4.7
15. University of California—Santa Barbara	4.6
16. New York University	4.6
University of Texas—Austin	4.6
University of Wisconsin—Madison	4.6
19. University of Massachusetts	4.5
University of Washington	4.5

ECONOMICS

UNIVERSITY-PROGRAM	SCORE
1. Massachusetts Institute of Technology	5.8
2. University of Wisconsin—Madison	5.5
3. University of Pennsylvania	5.4
4. Yale University	5.4
5. Harvard University	5.2
6. Stanford University	5.1
7. Princeton University	5.1
8. University of Chicago	5.0
University of Minnesota	5.0
10. University of Michigan	5.0
11. Carnegie-Mellon University	5.0
12. Columbia University	5.0
13. University of California—Berkeley	4.9
Northwestern University	4.9
15. University of Illinois—Urbana/Champaign	4.8
16. Cornell University	4.7
17. Virginia Polytechnic Institute	4.6
18. University of California—Los Angeles	4.6
19. Brown University	4.5
20. University of Virginia	4.4

GEOGRAPHY

UNIVERSITY-PROGRAM	SCORE
1. Ohio State University	5.5
2. University of California—Berkeley	5.3
3. University of Minnesota	5.3
4. Pennsylvania State University	5.3
5. Clark University	5.0
6. University of Wisconsin—Madison	5.0
7. University of Illinois—Urbana/Champaign	4.9
8. University of Wisconsin—Milwaukee	4.9
9. University of California—Los Angeles	4.8
University of Colorado	4.8
11. University of Washington	4.7
12. University of Hawaii	4.7
13. University of Nebraska	4.6
14. University of Iowa	4.6
Syracuse University	4.6
16. University of Georgia	4.5
17. Indiana University	4.4
18. Michigan State University	4.4
19. University of Kansas	4.3
20. University of Tennessee	4.1
Louisiana State University	4.1

HISTORY

UNIVERSITY-PROGRAM	SCORE
1. Yale University	5.5
2. University of California—Berkeley	5.4
3. Princeton University	5.4
4. University of Michigan	5.3
5. Harvard University	5.3
6. University of Chicago	5.1
7. University of California—Los Angeles	5.1
University of Wisconsin—Madison	5.1
9. University of Pennsylvania	5.0
10. University of North Carolina	5.0
Stanford University	5.0
12. Rutgers University	4.9
13. University of Texas—Austin	4.9
14. Cornell University	4.8
15. Johns Hopkins University	4.8
16. University of Virginia	4.7
17. Duke University	4.7
18. Brown University	4.7
19. Northwestern University	4.7
20. University of Illinois—Urbana/Champaign	4.6

POLITICAL SCIENCE

UNIVERSITY-PROGRAM	SCORE
1. University of Michigan	6.4
2. University of California—Berkeley	5.6
3. Yale University	5.4
4. Massachusetts Institute of Technology	5.1
5. University of Chicago	5.1
6. University of Wisconsin—Madison	5.1
Indiana University	5.1
8. Harvard University	5.0
Johns Hopkins University	5.0
10. Ohio State University	5.0
11. University of Minnesota	4.9
12. University of North Carolina	4.8
13. University of Wisconsin—Milwaukee	4.8
14. Princeton University	4.8
15. Northwestern University	4.7
16. University of California—Los Angeles	4.7
17. Cornell University	4.7
18. University of Iowa	4.6
19. Rutgers University	4.6
20. University of Texas—Austin	4.6

PSYCHOLOGY

UNIVERSITY-PROGRAM	SCORE
1. University of Wisconsin—Madison	4.5
2. University of Michigan	4.4
3. Stanford University	4.3
4. Massachusetts Institute of Technology	4.2
5. University of Pennsylvania	4.2
6. University of California—Los Angeles	4.2
7. University of Minnesota	4.1
8. University of California—Berkeley	4.1
9. University of Illinois—Urbana/Champaign	4.1
10. Indiana University	4.0
11. Yale University	4.0
12. University of California—San Diego	4.0
13. Harvard University	4.0
14. University of Chicago	4.0
15. Brown University	3.9
16. Princeton University	3.9
17. Carnegie-Mellon University	3.8
University of Washington	3.8
19. University of Oregon	3.8
University of Texas—Austin	3.8
21. Cornell University	3.8
22. Johns Hopkins University	3.8
23. University of Colorado	3.8
24. Columbia University	3.7
25. University of Connecticut	3.7

SOCIOLOGY

UNIVERSITY-PROGRAM	SCORE
1. University of Michigan	5.9
2. University of Wisconsin—Madison	5.8
3. Columbia University	5.0
Duke University	5.0
5. University of Chicago	5.0
6. Indiana University	4.8
7. University of California—Berkeley	4.8
8. University of North Carolina	4.8
9. Yale University	4.7
10. University of Washington	4.7
11. Harvard University	4.7
12. Stanford University	4.6
13. University of California—Los Angeles	4.6
14. University of Illinois—Urbana/Champaign	4.6
15. University of Minnesota	4.5
16. Washington State University	4.5
17. Princeton University	4.5
18. University of Texas—Austin	4.4
19. Cornell University	4.4
20. SUNY at Stony Brook	4.4
University of Pennsylvania	4.4

FISKE REPORT

HIGHEST RATED SCHOOLS

College	Total Score
Brown University*	14
Stanford University*	14
University of Virginia*	14
University of Colorado	13
Dartmouth College*	13
Haverford College*	13
Indiana University*	13
University of Massachusetts	13
University of North Carolina—Chapel Hill*	13
Oberlin College*	13
St. John's College*	13
University of Texas—Austin*	13
University of Vermont	13
University of Wisconsin—Madison*	13

OTHER SCHOOLS RECEIVING ACADEMICS SCORE OF 5

Amherst College
Bryn Mawr College
California Institute of Technology
University of California—Berkeley
University of Chicago
Barnard College
Columbia College
Cornell University
Hamilton College
Harvard University
University of Illinois—Urbana—Champaign
The Johns Hopkins University
Massachusetts Institute of Technology
University of Michigan
University of Pennsylvania
Princeton University
Smith College
Swarthmore College
Wellesley College
Wesleyan University
Williams College
Yale University

* Received Academics score of 5

APPENDIX C
VOCATIONAL SCHOOLS
A Reference by State

THE SEARCH

With so many people interested in and talking about vocational education and training, it's hard to understand the lack of a national data base on the subject. Finding all the alternatives in the vocational/technical arena will take some sleuthing on your part. The sources of the information cross many lines because of the sheer number of schools, some profit and some nonprofit.

You can start your search simply by checking the Yellow Pages. Most states and many counties operate vocational/technical schools or offer vocational curricula at junior colleges; just write the school system you're interested in for a catalog. You can also write to some nationally recognized, vocational education trade associations for guidance. Start with: the National Association of Trade and

Technical Schools, 2021 K Street NW, Washington, D.C. 20006; the Association of Independent Colleges and Schools, Suite 350, One Dupont Circle, Washington, D.C. 20036; the Southern Association of Colleges and Schools, 795 Peachtree Street NE, Atlanta, GA 30365; and the American Vocational Association, 2020 14 Street N., Arlington, VA.

Listed below are the addresses of the various state directors of vocational education, provided to us by the American Vocational Association. They can provide you with information about facilities in their states.

APPENDIX D

ADDRESSES OF VOCATIONAL EDUCATION SCHOOLS

Alabama
State Director, Divisional of
Vocational Education
State Department of Education
887 State Office Building
Montgomery, AL 36130
205/832-3364

Alaska
Career/Vocational Education
Administrator
State Department of Education
Alaska Office Building
Pouch F
Juneau, AK 99811
907/465-2980

Arizona
Deputy Superintendent and
Director of Vocational
Education
Special Program Services
1535 West Jefferson
Phoenix, AZ 85007
602/255-5343

Arkansas
Director for Vocational,
Technical and Adult
Education
State Department of Education
406 State Education Bldg., West
Capitol Mall
Little Rock, AR 72201
501/371-2165

California
Associate Superintendent for
    Vocational and Continuing
    Education
State Department of Education
721 Capitol Mall, 4th Floor
Sacramento, CA 95814
916/445-3314

Colorado
State Board for Community
    College and Occupational
    Education
Centennial Building, 2nd Floor
1313 Sherman Street
Denver, CO 80203
303/866-3071

Connecticut
Associate Commissioner/Director
Division of Vocational and Adult
    Education
State Department of Education
P.O. Box 2219
Hartford, CT 06115
203/566-7546

Delaware
Acting State Director of
    Vocational Education
State Department of Public
    Instruction
J. G. Townsend Building
P.O. Box 1402
Dover, DE 19901
302/736-4638

Washington, D.C.
Division of Career and
    Continuing Education
415 12th Street, N.W., Room 904
Washington, D.C. 20004
202/724-4184

Florida
Director, Division of Vocational
    Education
State Department of Education
Knott Building
Tallahassee, FL 32301
904/488-8961

Georgia
Associate Superintendent
Office of Vocational Education
State Department of Education
237 State Office Building
Atlanta, GA 30334
404/656-6711

Guam
Provost
Guam Community College
P.O. Box 23069
Guam Main Facility
Guam 96921
671/734-4311, Ext. 47 or 48

Hawaii
Acting State Director of
    Vocational Education
2327 Dole Street
Honolulu, HI 96822
808/948-7461

Idaho
State Administrator of Vocational
    Education
650 West State Street
Boise, ID 83720
208/334-216

Illinois
Assistant State Superintendent
Department of Adult, Vocational
    and Technical Education
Illinois State Board of Education
100 North First Street
Springfield, IL 62777
217/782-4627

Indiana
Acting Executive Director/State
    Director of Vocational
    Education
State Board of Vocational and
    Technical Education
401 Illinois Building
17 West Market Street
Indianapolis, IN 46204
317/232-1814

Iowa
Director of Career Education
Iowa Department of Public
    Instruction
Grimes State Office Building
Des Moines, IA 50319
515/281-4700

Kansas
Director of Vocational Education
State Department of Education
120 East Tenth Street
Topeka, KS 66612
913/296-3951

Kentucky
Assistant Superintendent for
    Vocational Education
State Department of Education
2011 Capital Plaza Tower
Frankfort, KY 40601
502/564-4286

Louisiana
Assistant State Superintendent
    Vocational Education
State Department of Education
Capitol Station—Box 44064
Baton Rouge, LA 70804
504/342-3524

Maine
Associate Commissioner
Bureau of Vocational Education
Department of Educational and
    Cultural Services
Education Building, Station 23
Augusta, ME 04333
207/289-2621

Maryland
Assistant State Superintendent
    Vocational-Technical
    Education
State Department of Education
200 W. Baltimore Street
Baltimore, MD 21201
301/659-2075

Massachusetts
Associate Commissioner
Division of Occupational
    Education
Quincy Center Plaza
1385 Hancock Street
Quincy, MA 02169
617/770-7350

Michigan
State Director
Vocational-Technical Education
    Service
State Department of Education
P.O. Box 30009
Lansing, MI 48909
517/373-3373

Minnesota
Assistant Commissioner
Division of Vocational-Technical
    Education
State Department of Education
564 Capitol Square Building
550 Cedar Street
St. Paul, MN 55101
612/296-3995

Mississippi
Vocational-Technical Education
State Department of Education
P.O. Box 771
Jackson, MS 39205
601/359-3088

Missouri
Assistant Commissioner and
    Director of Vocational
    Education
State Department of Elementary
    and Secondary Education
P.O. Box 480
Jefferson City, MO 65102
314/751-2660

Montana
Assistant State Superintendent
    for Vocational Education
    Service
Office of Public Instruction
106 State Capitol
Helena, MT 59620
406/449-2410

Nebraska
Assistant Commissioner for
    Vocational Education
State Department of Education
301 Centennial Mall South
P.O. Box 94987
Lincoln, NE 68509
402/471-2435

Nevada
State Director Vocational and
    Continuing Education
State Department of Education
400 West King Street, Capitol
    Complex
Carson City, NV 89710
702/885-3144

New Hampshire
Acting Chief
Division of Vocational-Technical
    Education
State Department of Education
105 Loudon Road
Concord, NH 03301
603/271-2452

New Jersey
Assistant Commissioner of
    Education and State
    Director of Vocational
    Education
State Department of Education
225 West State Street
Trenton, NJ 08625
609/292-6340

New Mexico
State Director of Vocational
    Education
State Department of Education
Education Building
Santa Fe, NM 87503
505/827-6511

New York
Assistant Commissioner for
    Occupational and
    Continuing Education
State Department of Education
99 Washington Avenue, Room
    1624
Albany, NY 12230
518/474-4688

North Carolina
Director
Division of Vocational Education
Department of Public Instruction
535 Education Building
Raleigh, NC 27611
919/733-7362

North Dakota
State Director Vocational
    Education
State Board of Vocational
    Education
State Capitol
Bismarck, ND 58505
701/224-2259

Ohio
Director
Division of Vocational Education
Ohio Department of Education
907 Ohio Departments Building
65 South Front Street
Columbus, OH 43215
614/466-3430

Oklahoma
State Director
Vocational and Technical
    Education
1515 West Sixth Avenue
Stillwater, OK 74074
405/377-2000, Ext. 200

Oregon
Assistant Superintendent
Division of Vocational Education
State Department of Education
700 Pringle Parkway, SE
Salem, OR 97310
503/378-2337

Pennsylvania
State Director
Vocational Education
State Department of Education
333 Market Street
P.O. Box 911
Harrisburg, PA 17108
717/787-5530

Puerto Rico
Acting Assistant Secretary
Vocational-Technical Education
State Department of Education
Box 759
Hato Rey, PR 00919
809/755-9128

Rhode Island
Deputy Assistant Commissioner
    for Vocational Education
State Department of Education
Roger Williams Building, Room
    222B
22 Hayes Street
Providence, RI 02908
401/277-2691

South Carolina
Director
Office of Vocational Education
State Department of Education
908 Rutledge Office Building
Columbia, SC 29201
803/758-5372

South Dakota
State Director
Division of Vocational-Technical
    Education
Richard F. Kneip Building
Pierre, SD 57501
605/773-3423

Tennessee
Assistant Commissioner
Division of Vocational Education
State Department of Education
200 Cordell Hull Building
Nashville, TN 37219
615/741-1716

Texas
Associate Commissioner for
  Occupational Education and
  Technology
Texas Education Agency
201 East 11th Street
Austin, TX 78701
512/834-4300

Utah
Administrator
Vocational Education Division
State Office of Education
250 East 5th South Street
Salt Lake City, UT 84111
801/533-5371

Vermont
State Director
Adult & Vocational-Technical
  Education
State Department of Education
State Office Building
Montpelier, VT 05602
802/828-3131

Virgin Islands
State Director
Vocational Education
Department of Education
P.O. Box 6640
Charlotte Amalie, VI 00801
809/744-3046

Virginia
Administrative Director
Vocational & Adult Education
State Department of Education
P.O. Box 6Q
Richmond, VA 23216
804/225-2073

Washington
Executive Director
Commission for Vocational
  Education
Building #17, Airdustrial Park
MS/LS-10
Olympia, WA 98504
206/753-5660

West Virginia
Assistant Superintendent
Bureau of Vocational, Technical
  and Adult Education
Building Six, Room B221
1900 Washington Street, East
Charleston, WV 25305
304/348-2346

Wisconsin
State Director
Wisconsin Board of Vocational,
  Technical and Adult
  Education
4802 Sheboygan Avenue, 7th
  Floor
P.O. Box 7874
Madison, WI 53707
608/266-1770

Wyoming
Assistant Superintendent
Vocational Planning Unit
State Department of Education
Hathaway Building
Cheyenne, WY 82002
307/777-7415

Samoa
State Director of Vocational
  Education
Department of Education
Government of American Samoa
P.O. Box 324
Pago Pago, Samoa 96799
684/633-5238

Executive Director of NASDVE
  & NVEPDC
200 Lamp Post Lane
Camp Hill, PA 17011
717/763-1120

Trust Territories of the Pacific
  Islands
Director Vocational Education
Department of Education
Headquarters
Saipan, Mariana Islands 96950
Saipan 9319-9428-9312

Acting Director of Vocational
  Education
Department of Education
Lower Base, Tanapaq
Saipan, CM 96950
782-9827

VOTRAKON—Director
USREP/JECOR
APO, New York 09038

Index

ABOUT THE AUTHORS

Dr. Marvin Cetron, president of Forecasting, International, Ltd., in Arlington, Virginia, is a pioneer in the areas of occupational and scientific forecasting. He teaches at American University, Georgia Tech and MIT, and lectures extensively throughout the world. His last book for McGraw-Hill, *Encounters with the Future*, received wide critical acclaim and has gone through multiple printings. Dr. Cetron has appeared on major national talk shows and is a favorite with the media.

Marcia Appel manages communication programs for a Fortune 500 computer services company in Minneapolis. She also has 13 years experience as a newspaper reporter and editor of business and women's magazines.